MIGHTY MOVIES

MOVIE POSTER ART FROM HOLLYWOOD'S
GREATEST ADVENTURE EPICS AND SPECTACULARS

WRITTEN AND COLLECTED BY LAWRENCE BASSOFF

Foreword with Jean Simmons

The participation of Ms. Jean Simmons is deeply appreciated.

ACKNOWLEDGMENTS
The Art Gallery Society of New South Wales, Sydney, Australia
Veronique Bernard, Harriet Greenberg, Katie Jacobs, Jo Jordan,
K & H Photo Lab, Peribo Pty Limited, Aaron Silverman,
Paul Thompson, John Truby, Joy Willis

Academic input: Dr. Richard B. Jewell, Associate Dean,
University of Southern California School of Cinema-Television

A great big thank you: Lindsay Granger

Also published by Lawrence Bassoff Collection:

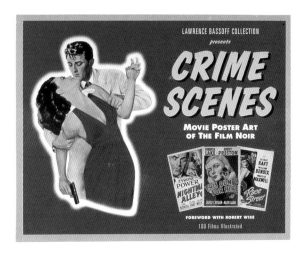

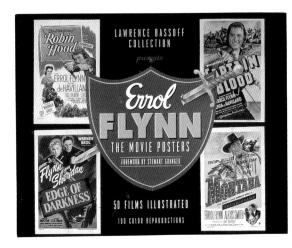

CRIME SCENES:
Movie Poster Art of The Film Noir
Foreword with Robert Wise
$35 U.S. / ISBN: 1-886310-11-4

ERROL FLYNN:
The Movie Posters
Foreword by Stewart Granger
$35 U.S. / ISBN: 1-886310-10-6

To order call: 1-(800)-247-6553 (Toll-free / 24-hours in U.S.)
Internet: http://www.bookmasters.com

DESIGN: Annmarie Dalton, Dalton Design, Santa Monica, CA
ART DIRECTION: Lawrence Bassoff
PHOTOGRAPHY: Tom Bickerstaff, Los Angeles, CA
LAYOUT: Karen Bowers, Curatorial Assistance, Los Angeles, CA
RESTORATION: Igor and Lara Edelman, Poster Restoration
Studio, Los Angeles, CA
PUBLISHING CONSULTANT: Tracy Marsh
RESEARCH CONSULTANT: Gary Grayson
PRODUCED BY Phoenix Offset, Hong Kong
Printed in China

Published by:
Lawrence Bassoff Collection, Incorporated
Post Office Box 5768
Beverly Hills, CA 90209-5768

Library of Congress Catalogue Card Number: 99-095159

ISBN: 1-886310-14-9

SAN: 298-4210

10 9 8 7 6 5 4 3 2 1

CONTENTS

Front cover detail—1935 pressbook

EPIC VERSUS SPECTACLE

In today's Hollywood, the epic is ordinary. Production and marketing budgets are staggering—but so is boxoffice. The global cultural and commercial impact of the motion picture industry itself overshadows the significance of any particular film, no matter how titanically successful. The heretofore Hollywood-heralded "Cast of Thousands!" is migrating behind the camera in an optical revolution won by digital illusion. The Industry is retooling from the ground—and thrills—up and the emphasis, as ever, is on bigger.

But in *their day*, the Hollywood adventure epics and spectaculars depicted in this book were the biggest of the big. And they were made by the biggest of the big. *Motion picture events*, Hollywood called them. Years in the making and, usually, years in the waiting for them to be completed and released. From *The Birth of a Nation* in 1915 through the birth of Cinemascope in 1953 and beyond to the super-spectacles of the 1960s, their legacy spawned popular definitions of grandeur and scale.

In an era when pageantry was measured by how much production value—human, animal, or otherwise—could be displayed on a set or location and physically photographed, what could possibly be "bigger than *Ben-Hur*"? If the twentieth was truly "The American Century", then the movie miracles Hollywood created and exported to the world should be regarded as artistic technological expressions of a modern industrialized democracy.

Yes, exploiting size has always been the name of the game in Hollywood epic filmmaking. But, beware—not all "epics" in this book are alike. That's because some "epics," like our example, RKO's 1935 *She*, actually should be called "spectacles." What's the difference between an epic and a spectacle? Author John Cary, in his 1974 book, *Spectacular: The Story of Epic Films*, makes this discrimination:

"Now is the best moment to make a distinction between film epic and film spectacular, although the two are so often combined that the terms have become almost interchangeable. Every epic is a spectacle, but not every spectacle achieves the epic. On the screen, the epic is dramatic; the spectacular is visual. The epic sublimates narrative into something loftier and full of resonance, while the spectacular functions mostly as an elaborate illustration of a given text. When an epic fails, it becomes a spectacle. When a spectacle fails, it becomes cinema at its most pretentious or at its most grotesque."

Thus enlightened, please enjoy a nostalgic tour of the splendor, savagery and spectacle of the screen epics that staggered the world!

Window card (1935—trimmed, border loss)

Title card (1953)

FOREWORD
TEA FOR TWO JEAN SIMMONS

There they are, standing together in the cozy Southern California kitchen, the two Jean Simmons. They're thrashing out in which room of this bright, rambling and comfy home we should have tea. I'm seeing them together for the first time today and the similarities are striking.

"Identical height?" I ask upon meeting them.

"I'm taller," says Jean Simmons, arching upward ever so mockingly. "She's the one who's shrinking."

"I'm here to aggravate her," smiles the other Jean Simmons, moving closer so I can compare their heights. "I've had years of practice."

"I give her a bad time and she gives me a bad time," says the first Jean, cinching a cozy into a steaming teapot so prodigious only a British expatriate would chance wielding it around guests. "But it's all in fun," she chirps. "That's what makes us a good team."

The two Jean Simmons laugh.

There is, of course, only one Jean Simmons. The "other Jean" is actress Jo Jordan. In between her own roles, Jo has acted numerous ones in Jean's life, most often as her production associate and stand-in since Jean first arrived in the United States in 1951 to star in *Androcles and the Lion*. No, "Jo-Jo" isn't Jean's doppelganger facially. Let's just say they each take up an uncannily similar unit of space. (See respective photos on pages 10–11.) Which is exactly how Jo was "discovered" by Jean's then-husband, film star Stewart Granger (1913–1993).

Jo and "Jimmy" (as Granger was known to friends) were performing together earlier that same year in MGM's *The Light Touch*, which was written and directed by Jean's much-later-to-be second husband, Richard Brooks (1912–1992). Throughout production, Granger kept remarking how much Jo reminded him of his

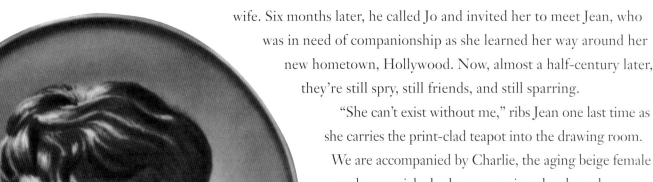

Spartacus one-sheet (1960—detail)

wife. Six months later, he called Jo and invited her to meet Jean, who was in need of companionship as she learned her way around her new hometown, Hollywood. Now, almost a half-century later, they're still spry, still friends, and still sparring.

"She can't exist without me," ribs Jean one last time as she carries the print-clad teapot into the drawing room. We are accompanied by Charlie, the aging beige female cocker spaniel who becomes miraculously perky once the cappuccino-flavored muffins start circulating.

The real purpose of this gathering is to discuss Jean's central involvement in a number of major British and Hollywood historical dramas and spectaculars from 1947 to 1960. Jo has kindly consented to join us to jog Jean's memory and her own. But first, a little background.

FROM CRICKLEWOOD TO HOLLYWOOD

In his book *The Great Movie Stars: The International Years*, David Shipman begins his entry on Jean Simmons with this assessment: "Jean Simmons has always been taken for granted. As a child player in Britain she was expected to be one of the best child players and she was; she was expected to become a big international name and she did. In Hollywood for over twenty years she was given good roles because she was reliable, and she played them, and most of them, beautifully, and got good notices, and was liked . . . she's not a competent actress, she's a very good one—by Hollywood standards a great one . . ."

That child player with the heavy expectations was born on January 31, 1929, the youngest of the three girls and a boy born to 1912 Olympic gymnastics bronze medalist Charles Simmons and his wife, Winnifred Ada Loveland Simmons, of Cricklewood, London. Fourteen-year-old Jean had just enrolled at Aida Foster

School of Dancing when an acting opportunity suddenly loomed up.

"I was at the school for only two weeks when Mrs. Foster said 'I'd like to take you to a movie studio to meet director Val Guest,'" recalls Jean. "We went, I met Mr. Guest, and I read a few lines they gave me about 'bloated capitalists' or something. The next thing I knew I was playing Margaret Lockwood's sister in the movie *Give Us the Moon* (1944). I was paid five pounds a day. Five pounds a day for thirty days."

"Five pounds a day for thirty days" quickly compounded into three more 1944 film roles (*Mr. Emmanuel*, *Kiss the Bride Goodbye*, *Meet Sexton Blake*), a career-priming contract with J. Arthur Rank Studios, and the start of a quarter century stand as one of the most respected and beautiful leading ladies of Hollywood.

After earning acclaim for her performances in such post-World War II British cinema classics as David Lean's *Great Expectations* (1946—as the haughty beauty, Estella) and Laurence Olivier's production of *Hamlet* (1948—Best Actress at the Venice Film Festival and a Best Supporting Actress Academy Award Nomination at age 19 for Ophelia), Jean married Granger in 1950. The pair moved to Hollywood the next year.

In addition to the period pieces she'll be recollecting, Jean also starred in such major Hollywood features as: *The Actress* (1953—her favorite filmmaking experience thanks to director George Cukor); *Guys and Dolls* (1955—mogul Samuel Goldwyn praised her performance by saying he was "glad Grace Kelly hadn't been available for the role after all"); *Elmer Gantry* (1960—Sister Sharon Falconer ranks with her

Crassus (Laurence Olivier), wealthy and powerful patrician who defeats the gladiator-slave rebels in "Spartacus," covets Varinia (Jean Simmons), wife of the rebel leader. She remains loyal to her heroic husband.

Jean Simmons, Laurence Olivier

very best work); *The Happy Ending* (1969—a Best Actress Academy Award nomination in a role written and directed by Jean's by-then second husband Brooks).

JEAN SIMMONS RECALLS:

Great Expectations (1946)
"I was the only girl they used to do a lot of screen tests with a lot of boys. When it came time for production, they cast Anthony Wager and simply said the role of Estella was mine. I just loved making the film. I couldn't wait to get to the studio everyday. As you may recall, I had to walk up and down the stairs holding a lit candle. One time my organza skirt caught on fire and Anthony ripped it off me just before I was burned."

Laurence Olivier's *Hamlet* (1948)
"I had never done Shakespeare. I hated it at school because they made it so boring. I was about to shoot another film at Pinewood Studios when I was told to study the part of Ophelia with acting teacher Molly Terraine. So, I rehearsed the part and Larry (Olivier) came to my dressing room to hear me read it. I was petrified, of course. I mean, there I was, a teenager standing in the corner of some dressing room, waiting to go on for the great Laurence Olivier. Larry signaled and we began. In the middle of the scene I heard a terrible 'Bang!' Larry had smacked the wall with his hand, trying to rattle me, I suppose. I acted like I didn't hear it, finished the scene and got the part. Larry proved to be a wonderful colleague and friend over the years."

Androcles and The Lion (1952)

"This was my first Hollywood movie and I was delighted to be working with Victor Mature for the first time. He was such a gentleman and he so wanted to be taken seriously as an actor. And dear Robert Newton was such a gem to act with, bless his heart."

Young Bess (1953)

"Charles Laughton, who played King Henry VIII, was always great fun to be around. He was rehearsing for the play *John Brown's Body* and we used to sit on the floor in his dressing room during breaks and listen to him read his lines. The costumes were so breathtaking in *Young Bess.* Jimmy (Granger) and I were so much in love then that our romantic scenes together were a piece of cake."

Luxurious living and sensual pleasures were the rule for the Roman patrician. In this scene from "Spartacus," Gracchus (Charles Laughton) and Batiatus (Peter Ustinov) enjoy a private feast with two slave-women.

Jill Jarmyn, Peter Ustinov, Charles Laughton, Jo Jordan

The Robe (1953)

"Production of *The Robe* was very difficult. The then-new Cinemascope process (Ed. Note: *The Robe* was the first Cinemascope feature) required a lot of extra lights so we were broiling for the entire shoot. The other problem with Cinemascope was the blocking of the scenes. Because the depth of field was so shallow, we actors were always being stationed across the wide screen as if we were in a police line-up. Richard (Brooks) used to say Cinemascope was 'designed for the funeral of a snake.'"

Desiree (1954)

"I'd seen Marlon Brando on Broadway in *A Streetcar Named Desire* and I thought he was such a talented actor and such a beautiful man. I was in complete awe of him.

My problem during *Desiree* was that I was more inclined to watch Marlon playing Napoleon than to attend to my own acting of the scene. His behavior in the scenes was so fascinating that I couldn't take my eyes off him."

Spartacus (1960)

"I so enjoyed working with Kirk Douglas, director Stanley Kubrick and that dream cast. To work with Larry Olivier and Charles Laughton again and, of course, dear Peter Ustinov. Prior to filming a scene with both Charles and Peter, they each pulled me aside out of earshot of the other and gently instructed me to 'just keep your eyes on me during the scene.'"

"Another memorable story from the *Spartacus* shoot involved the crucifixion scene at the end after the slave rebellion has been defeated. It was a very difficult process to tie Kirk as Spartacus onto his cross and then raise the cross upright with him tied on it and then get it into the ground and secure it with him still tied on it, etc. To make matters worse, it was a broiling hot day.

After what seemed like an eternity, they finally got Kirk's cross into position. A moment later, the first assistant director looked at his watch and called 'Lunch!' With Kirk still hanging on the cross, we all wordlessly started walking off the set as if we were going to leave him dangling there. Kirk really took it marvelously since as the producer he also could have sacked us on the spot for our spontaneous prank!"

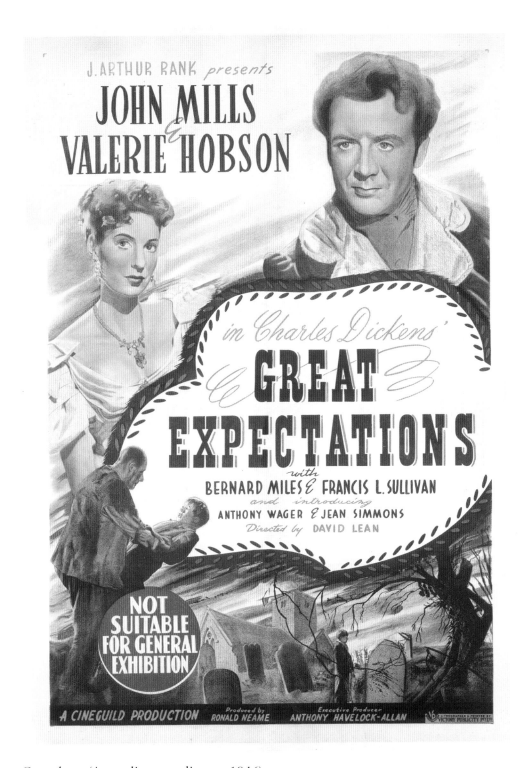

One-sheet (Australian—on linen—1946)

Daybill (1948)

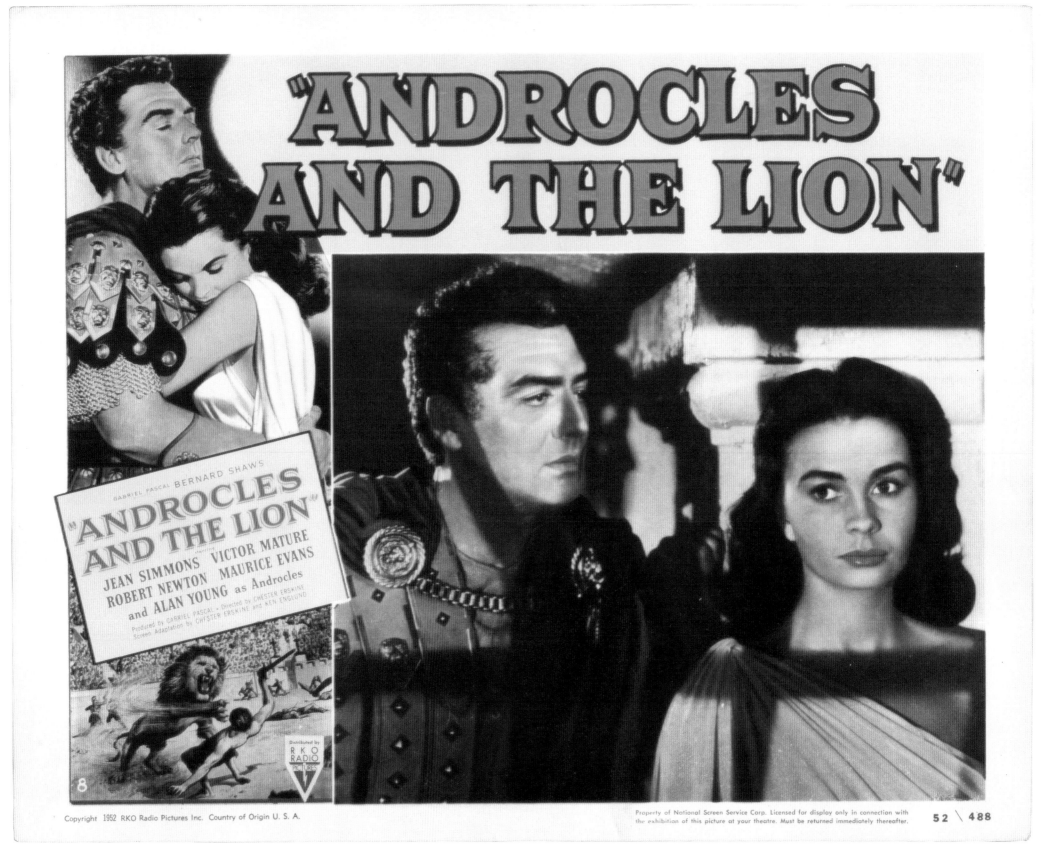

Victor Mature, Jean Simmons (1953 lobby card)

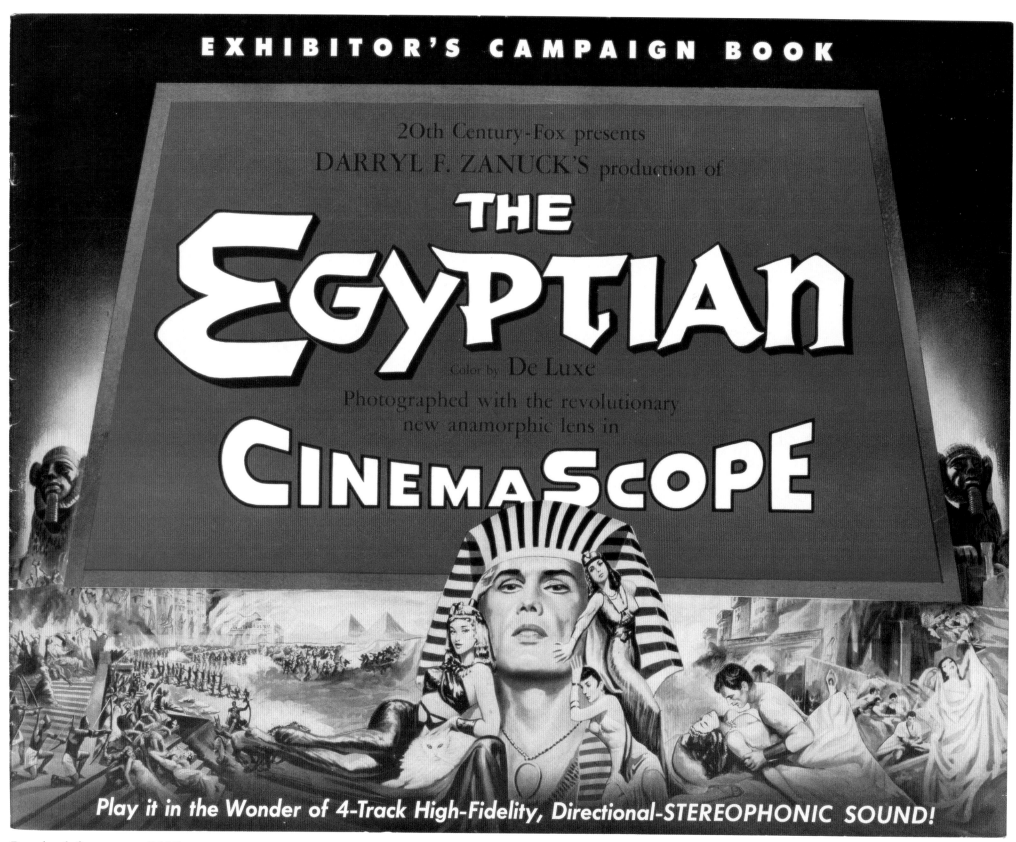

Pressbook front cover (1954)

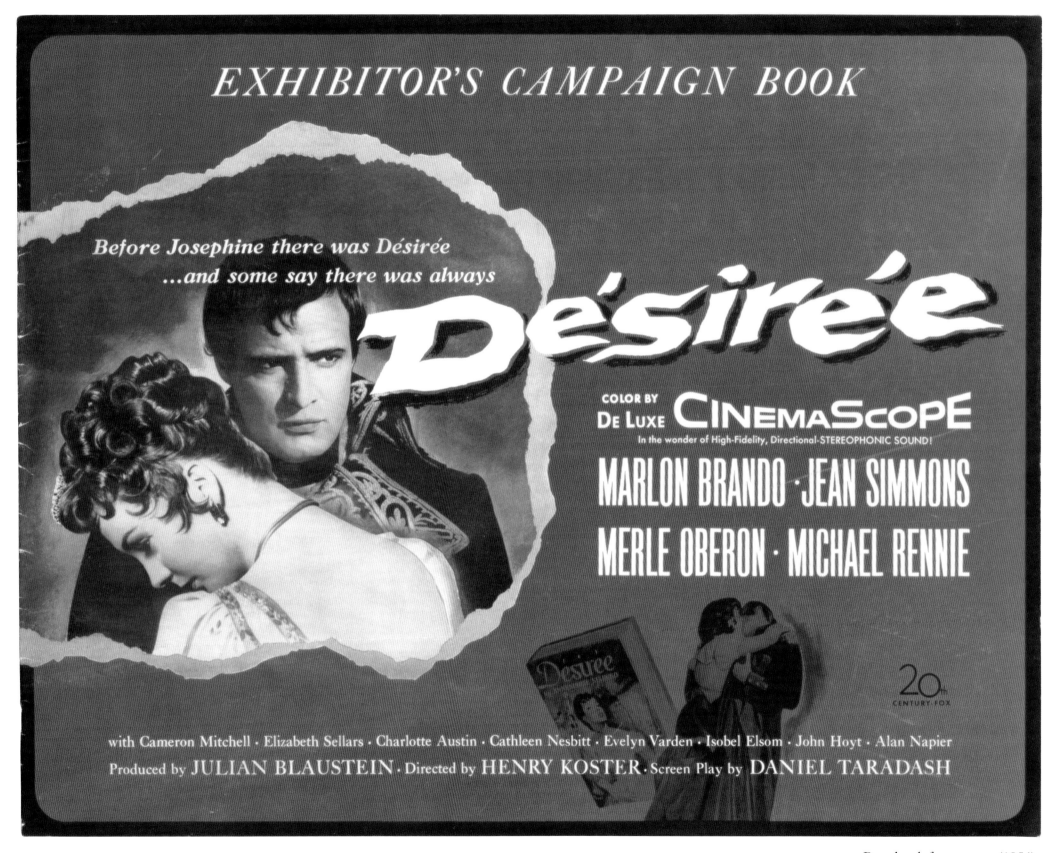

Pressbook front cover (1954)

One-sheet (1958—unrestored)

One-sheet detail (1958)

Title card (1958)

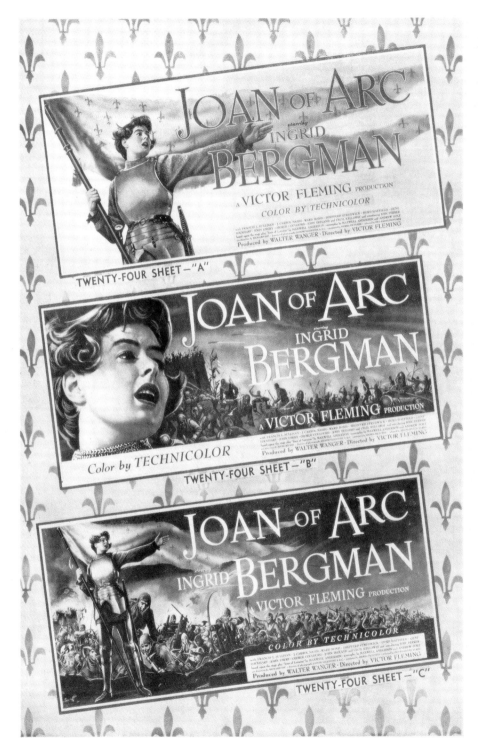

Pressbook detail (1948)

GLOSSARY OF MOVIE POSTER TERMINOLOGY

With the exception of a handful of international pieces, all the movie posters, lobby cards, and related promotional memorabilia in this book are American in origin.

Until the 1980s, a large variety of movie poster and lobby display items were made available for a nominal charge to movie theatres by either the movie companies directly or through National Screen Service. Today, the selection is limited to one-sheets, standees, and infrequently-issued lobby card sets.

Promotional booklets called *pressbooks* were distributed free of charge to theatres well in advance of a film's release. Printed on heavy-coated stock, they usually contained camera-ready ads or *mats*, publicity stories, and promotional and merchandising campaign strategies. More importantly, they served as catalogues for ordering movie poster material, which was often depicted on the back cover. These items were targeted to reach pedestrians who walked past theatre lobbies, local storefronts, or billboards.

The juxtaposition of the poster selection spread from the *Joan of Arc* pressbook on page 12 and the actual color lobby card on this page (which is depicted in black and white in the spread) illustrates the catalogue function of the pressbook. The uniform configurations of the plethora of items available allowed theatres to construct frames or sandwich boards into which they would rotate these standard sizes as releases played off.

The following poster formats are discussed and depicted in this book:

Ingrid Bergman (1948 lobby card)

One-sheet poster (27″ x 41″ / 675mm x 1025mm): The one-sheet is the most popular and well-known American movie poster size. Until the mid-1960s, they were printed on a porous, uncoated paper and machine folded into 11″ x 14″ rectangles for easy shipping. Today, one-sheets are printed on glossy, coated stock and shipped rolled. Up to four different styles (Style A, B, C, or D) could be printed for each release. When a film was re-released, the original one-sheet art would often be reproduced in a one or two-color version.

Half-sheet poster (22″ x 28″ / 550mm x 700mm): A horizontal rectangular poster which was printed on a heavy card stock and shipped either folded or rolled. Often the artwork would be identical to the title lobby card of the lobby card set, though more than one style half-sheet style was often printed.

Insert poster (14″ x 36″ / 350mm x 900mm): A narrow vertical poster, which was also printed on heavy card stock and often machine-folded into a rectangle for shipping.

Window card (14″ x 22″ / 350mm x 900mm): Window cards were printed on heavy card stock or cardboard and featured a blank strip at the top for imprinting the name of the local theatre. They came in a variety of other sizes—*jumbo*, *mini*, and *midget*—and were placed in storefront windows, on bulletin boards, etc.

Pressbook detail (1938)

Lobby card (11″ x 14″ / 275mm x 350mm): Lobby cards were traditionally printed on heavy card stock in sets of eight. The top card, or *title card*, was a full-blown miniature movie poster with artwork and billing identical or similar to that of a half-sheet. These are typically the most sought after by collectors. The other seven cards, which were often trimmed with colorful *border art* depicting title logos and billing, featured tinted posed publicity shots or scenes from the film. A card without a likeness of one of the leads or featured supporting players (i.e., a crowd or battle scene) is referred to as a *dead card*.

From the early 1960s until the mid-1990s, lobby card sets were simply 11″ x 14″ color stills printed on coated card stock. Since the mid-1980s, U.S. lobby card set production has been drastically reduced. Border art, however, has made a welcome return in many of the handsomely-printed contemporary British lobby card sets.

Daybill (14″ x 30″ / 350mm x 750mm): A daybill is a narrow poster printed exclusively in Australia for use in Australia and New Zealand. Six inches shorter than inserts, the majority of vintage daybills were printed as stone lithographs until as late as the mid-1970s. The layout and design of numerous vintage daybills were copied from the similarly vertically-configured U.S. 3-sheet art. Daybills printed in the 1930s measured 15″ x 40″ (375mm x 900mm) and are often referred to as *long daybills*.

Belgian posters: Belgian posters are very colorful offset pieces which were printed in vertical and horizontal configurations. They feature the film's title in French, Flemish, and, sometimes, English. They also have a window-card type strip for local theatre imprinting. Smaller posters were usually stapled, stamped, and dropped in the mail, which accounts for canceled stamps being glued to numerous vintage Belgian pieces.

Other relevant movie poster terminology:

Key art: The central illustration or photograph around which an ad or movie poster campaign is based.

Duotone: A two-ink printing process, usually black and one color, featured on many Warner Bros. one-sheets of the mid-1930s to late 1940s and on the reissue posters of most other studios through the early 1960s.

Linenbacking: A restoration procedure where posters are cleaned, reinforced by mounting on rice paper and then hand or machine mounted on canvas, which is referred to as "linen."

Reissue: A subsequent re-release of a film after its original release. Poster material was usually reprinted in one or two colors to accompany this release and such material is usually denoted with the year and the word "reissue," i.e., 1947 reissue. On the posters themselves, this would be printed in the lower right corner as: "R 47."

Standee: A dye-cut, free-standing cardboard lobby display, often deployed to tout an upcoming movie. Standees are usually five to six feet (1500mm to 1800mm) high and employ key art from the overall ad campaign. Standees faded out in the early 1960s, but came roaring back to more-elaborate-than-ever theatre life in the mid-1980s to promote the host of action movie franchises and their respective sequels (*Die Hard, Batman*, etc.)

Stone lithography: A now-obsolete printing process whereby the poster image was "burned" into a stone plate resulting in a less-saturated, textured application of ink during printing.

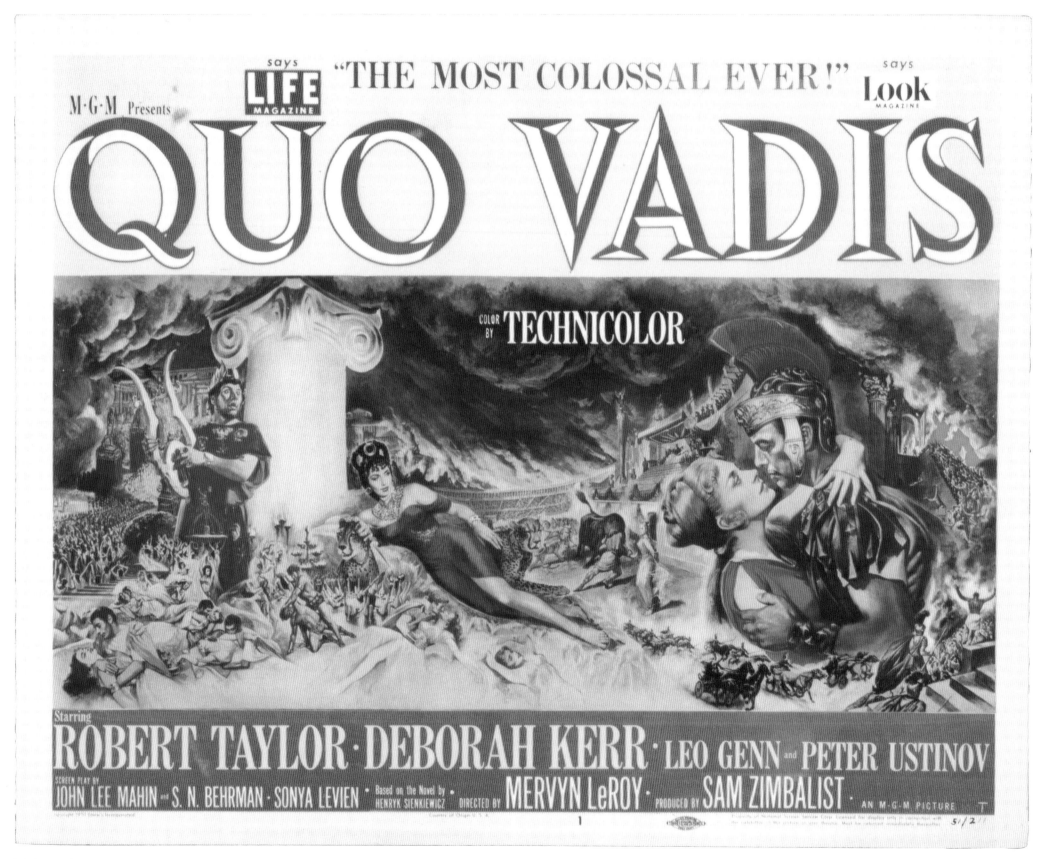

Title card (1951)

INTRODUCTION
A BOOK ABOUT BEING BIGGER THAN *BEN-HUR*

Mighty Movies—Movie Poster Art from Hollywood's Greatest Adventure Epics and Spectaculars is the first genre retrospective collection of movie poster art from Hollywood sound era historical and costume adventure pageants ever published. It employs original movie poster art and related memorabilia from the period 1900 to 1970 to trace and illustrate the evolution, zenith, and decline of the event-style screen spectacles for which Hollywood became globally famous.

In so doing, the book illustrates and profiles forty-one major feature film examples from the period 1932 to 1970 and illustrates a further fifty examples in gallery fashion and run-of-the-book illustration. Finally, *Mighty Movies* offers a 16-page supplement summarizing and illustrating the short and colorful history of the muscleman-driven *sword and sandal spectacles* produced in Europe during the period 1957 to 1965.

Like our inaugural volumes, *Errol Flynn—The Movie Posters* (1995) and *Crime Scenes—Movie Poster Art of The Film Noir* (1997), *Mighty Movies* utilizes movie poster art in an illustrative and artifactual sense. Not only does it provide a vintage commercial art platform for recalling these films, but it also describes and compares the various studio in-house art department poster styles by providing numerous examples from each.

And, like the latter books, this work is an expression of the intensification of interest in the United States, Europe, Latin America, and Australia since 1989 in collecting, studying, and trading in vintage posters from Hollywood movies of all

Broadway (1951)

international origins. In the latter year, the exposure and celebration of movie posters was dramatically enhanced by the first of a continuing series of auctions begun in Los Angeles by Camden House Auctioneers and practiced now by Christies, Sotheby's, Butterfield and Butterfield, and others in London, New York, Los Angeles, Boston, Sydney and Melbourne.

Outstanding individual auction prices are constantly trumpeted in the media. At this printing, the reigning auction champion is a one-sheet from *The Mummy* (1933) which sold for $453,000 in New York in March, 1997. Less stratospherically-priced items routinely change hands from $100 to $2,500 with numerous pieces selling for $10,000 to $25,000. What had once been a sleepy hobby has become an active collectibles niche market, a transition bemoaned by the collector who recalls the availability and prices of the early days.

Concurrent with the rise of the auction scene has been the maturation of the art of movie poster restoration. Torn, soiled, and incomplete posters of any size (including full billboard 24-sheets) can now be transformed into major works of movie poster art by the truly alchemic techniques of the better restoration studios. Igor and Lara Edelman of Poster Restoration Studio of Los Angeles are responsible for all of the restored pieces featured here.

Outside the auction houses, a lively traffic in posters is ongoing in private sales, on ever-expanding Internet websites, at regional memorabilia shows, and within the

pages of the bi-monthly newspaper *Movie Collectors World*.

Finally, apart from an opening overview of our subject, it is impossible to concisely summarize the wealth of data and opinion in print on various aspects of epic and spectacular film. While the final selection of titles illustrated and evaluated is representative of the genre, it is not all-inclusive. Certain major examples may be unrepresented for which we apologize.

INTEREST AT AN EARLY AGE

The obsessions underlying *Mighty Movies* took root during a youth spent preoccupied with the Hollywood movies and related popular culture of the mid-1950s through the late 1960s. Early exposure to American history through the *World Book* encyclopedia and pervasive kiddie culture phenomena like Walt Disney's *Davy Crockett, King of the Wild Frontier* (1955) and Revolutionary War-set *Johnny Tremain* (1957) synergized well with other collecting interests: *Marx* toy soldiers; *Topps* baseball cards; *DC*, *Harvey*, and *Classics Illustrated* comic books; *Mattel* 'Shoot 'Em Shell' cap pistols.

A boyhood in Queens, New York, and Long Island also meant easy grandmother-assisted access to Manhattan roadshow engagements of *Ben-Hur* (1959), *Spartacus* (1960), and *El Cid* (1961). The soundtrack albums from the latter trio withstood scores of serial stackings on our *Webcor* monaural record player and succeeding *Fisher*-amplifier-*Garrard*-turntable-*KLH*-speakers early component stereo.

An appreciation of the classic films of the 1930s and 1940s was cultivated by broadcasts of the gems of the studio film libraries on local New York television. It was in these repeat offerings of *Captain Blood* (1935), *The Adventures of Robin Hood*

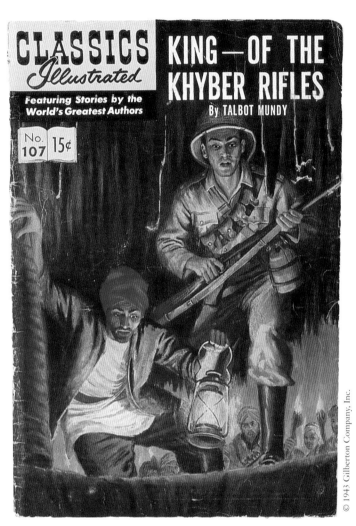

© 1943 Gilberton Company, Inc.

Front cover (1960s reprint)

(1938), and *The Sea Hawk* (1940) that I was introduced to Errol Flynn. Here was history come to life, a lithe, laughing, indomitable screen swashbuckler too charming and complete to be conjured by an eight-year-old. Even before knowing Flynn's name, the opening fanfare of any Erich Wolfgang Korngold or Max Steiner score for a Flynn film would rivet me to our *Zenith* television for the next two hours. I was hooked on Hollywood historical films from then on.

The last significant influence to prime the collecting spirit was my 1969 discovery of the bound volumes of the freshly-published *New York Times Film Reviews* (1913–1968) in the library at Cornell University in Ithaca, New York. The 1,142-page index allowed me to unearth the reviews of practically any movie I could remember. This process of, if you will, *movie memory authentication* kept me poring over the tablet-like tomes for hours and then, years. My parents even bought me a set as a graduation gift. The roster of favorite film titles which would first whet my movie poster collecting appetite was compiled by this ritual of film memory/film review verification.

WHERE DO THESE MOVIE POSTERS COME FROM?

The vintage U.S. movie poster paper currently in circulation was produced by either the major studios and independent distributors themselves or by an organization called National Screen Service, which was formed by Herman Robbins in 1926 to print and distribute posters and related materials for the studios.

For decades after, movie poster exchanges dotted the country. As a number of the independent ones went out of business in the late 1950s and 1960s, their stocks of

used and uncirculated posters, lobby cards, pressbooks, etc., were purchased by dealers. A niche market was born. While National Screen Service continues to distribute posters today, several of the major studios returned to printing and distributing their own posters in the early 1980s.

A number of the pieces in this book originated in a 1961 buyout of over one million items from two defunct exchanges, one from Canada, one from the southern United States. For the next three decades, this trove formed the mother lode of a Manhattan-based shop. I'd heard about the store from a college friend and, with my Errol Flynn-Tyrone Power-Stewart Granger want list in hand, I went there to investigate. It took several tantalizing—and frustrating — visits to prove to the client-selective proprietor that I was Hollywood-savvy enough to make intelligent poster requests. *Finally*, I was permitted to be a customer. There were so many stacks of posters piled around that if you found one you liked and set it down just nearby, there was a good chance you'd never find it again. Lost—before your very eyes—in the sea of machine-folded rectangles. The good old days.

From the 1920s into the late 1960s, most of the studios relied on in-house advertising and publicity departments to design the promotional materials which were printed at the latter plants. With a few famous exceptions like Norman Rockwell, anonymous staff commercial illustrators created archives full of original movie poster art: portraits, epic scenes, hand-lettered logos and title treatments, etc. Virtually none of this original artwork exists today.

As discussed, to keep the materials flowing for the distribution of as many as fifty releases per major studio per year, in-house graphic styles were developed which facilitated production line design and completion. Numerous examples from all the major studios are represented here. There is a definite pecking order among

Front cover (1960s reprint)

the differing studio styles. The richly-saturated color of the Paramount and RKO offset and stone lithograph posters from Morgan Lithograph are the most handsome and accomplished. (Compare Paramount's *A Connecticut Yankee in King Arthur's Court*, page 120, with RKO's *The Princess and The Pirate*, page 127.) Twentieth Century-Fox also printed in stone and offset lithography styles. (See *Captain from Castile*, page 52, and *The Black Rose*, page 55, for outstanding offset examples.) Their stone lithographs printed by Tooker Litho Company are especially prized.

Despite a plethora of collectible titles and stars, Metro-Goldwyn-Mayer posters tend to be all of a piece stylistically, repeatedly featuring tightly-illustrated star portraiture on a white background. (See *Northwest Passage*, page 50; *Scaramouche*, page 66; *The Prodigal*, page 129; *Young Bess*, page 133.)

Warner Bros. utilized a photography-based style and cheaper two and three color printing for its one-sheets from the mid-1930s through the early 1960s. They, too, have a production line sameness which their increasing antiquity and the quality of the stars depicted has partially overcome. (See *Land of the Pharaohs*, page 78; *Helen of Troy*, page 80; *The Flame and The Arrow*, page 122.)

Universal Pictures developed a 1940s' poster style which often featured seemingly disembodied, photographic head shot likenesses of stars and key supporting players floating against a background of billing and copy. (See *Sudan* for a less slavish example of the above, page 131.) Its 1950s' output as Universal-International featured superior illustration. (See *Sign of the Pagan*, page 130.) Columbia Pictures employed Morgan lithography very successfully in the 1930s. An outstanding later Columbia poster is *Salome* on page 129.

Rescued after the sea battle (1900 Klaw and Erlanger *Ben-Hur* stage production program detail)

HOLLYWOOD LOVES HISTORY

The kernel of curiosity which attracted early cinema patrons to half-minute Kinetoscope film strips like Edison's *The Execution of Mary, Queen of Scots* (1895) is the same curiosity the motion picture industry would target to attract audiences to epic films like the ones illustrated in this restrospective.

BIG BOOK, BIG MOVIE

The rise of the motion picture was predicated upon the principle that the cinema could capture people, objects, and settings (real or otherwise) and represent them as lifelike moving photographic images in the viewer's local peepshow parlor or theatre. This plastic visual component distinguished the fledgling art form from the epic poetry, literature, and various forms of theatre from which mass storytelling had evolved.

In picking up where audience imaginations left off, however, silent filmmakers shouldered increasingly greater responsibility to deliver increasingly more elaborate thrills. They rose to this challenge by spending larger sums of money to produce longer films for which they charged higher ticket prices. Popular historical novels, like Henryk Sienkiewicz's (1846–1916) 1897 magnum opus *Quo Vadis?*, were ideal pre-sold fodder for screen exploitation, a pattern the film industry would repeat for decades of epics to come. When the Astor Theatre in Manhattan raised admission from fifteen cents to an unparalleled one dollar and fifty cents for its heavily-promoted, "legitimate" engagement of Enrico Guazzoni's 1912 two-hour version of *Quo Vadis?*, the age of the event-style historical epic formally arrived—and Hollywood took notice.

Douglas Fairbanks, Enid Bennett (*Robin Hood*—1922)

SILENT PREDECESSORS (1914–1927)

The adventure epics and spectaculars of the period of this study (1932–1970) drew their inspiration and expertise from the seminal silent epics of the following filmmakers: D.W. Griffith (*Judith of Bethulia, The Clansman/ The Birth of a Nation, Intolerance, Orphans of the Storm, America*); Cecil B. DeMille (*The Ten Commandments, The King of Kings*); Sergei Eisenstein (*Potemkin, October*); Abel Gance (*Napoleon*); Giovanni Pastrone (*Cabiria*); Fred Niblo (*Ben-Hur*). The popularity of the silent genre was also established by the swashbuckling acrobatic charm of its greatest star, Douglas Fairbanks (*The Mark of Zorro, The Three Musketeers, Robin Hood, The Thief of Baghdad, The Black Pirate*).

Griffith and DeMille jump-started the epic cycle by marshaling the financing (including, often, their own) to mount their still-gargantuan blockbusters. Here, Hollywood learned in hurry-up fashion how to research and recreate whole cultures to order: structures, vehicles, clothing, hair styles, weapons, food, manners, battle tactics—the works. Low profile assistant and second unit directing assignments meant de facto field generalship of recreations nearly as epic as the actual events themselves.

In the sound era, as we shall see, the epic remained the domain of the signature producer with the clout to secure the budgets necessary: Alexander Korda (*The Four Feathers, The Thief of Baghdad*); David O. Selznick (*Gone With the Wind, Duel in the Sun*); Darryl F. Zanuck (*Lloyds of London, In Old Chicago*).

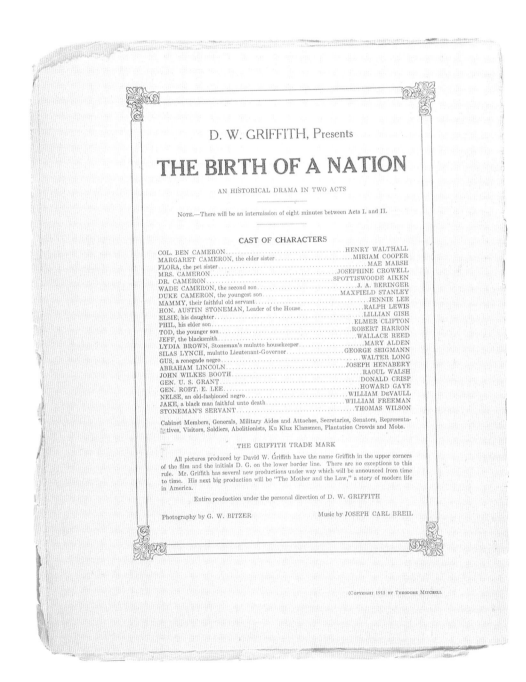

Program detail (1915)

Program detail (1915)

Ramon Novarro as Ben-Hur (1925)

Program cover (1925)

Charlton Heston, Christopher Rhodes (*El Cid* 1961 borderless roadshow lobby card)

TRIAL BY COMBAT
FOUR EPIC ENGAGEMENTS

No matter the sweep of the story, epic and spectacular films often grind to a multimillion dollar halt to focus on the enactment of one critical battle. *The moment of truth. The final reckoning. The fight to the finish.*

The only special effects employed in these four still-crunching chunks of virtuoso action filmmaking are the months of arduous weapons training and precise fight choreography accomplished by the stars themselves. For those who like their epic moviewatching dessert first, we offer the following epic engagements.

El Cid (1961) (Screen time: 4:21)

It's savage poetry in motion as Rodrigo Diaz de Bivar/El Cid (Charlton Heston) and Don Martin (Christopher Rhodes) square off in an 11th century single combat joust to the death to determine sovereignty over the medieval Spanish city of Calahorra. After withstanding three lance-splintering charges, Rodrigo is brutally unhorsed. In the film, the dazed and disarmed Rodrigo uses his charger's saddle to fend off Don Martin's sword blows until he can locate a weapon and strike back. In the lobby card pictured, he uses a shield. (See *El Cid*, pages 98–101.)

Spartacus (1960) (Screen time: 3:52)

A standard ancient Roman gladiatorial pairing was the cruel mismatch of *secutor*; the short range Thracian sword and shield, versus *retiarius*, the longer range trident-and-net combination. While the story circumstances of this 73 B.C. clash are tragic,

Kirk Douglas, Woody Strode (*Spartacus* 1960 lobby card—detail)

the encounter is electrifying. Stripped to a loincloth and poised behind his sword and a pie plate-sized shield, Spartacus (Kirk Douglas) crouches into a crab-like defensive posture to protect his torso from the height and reach advantage of towering opponent Draba (Woody Strode). (See *Spartacus*, pages 94–95.)

The Vikings (1958) (Screen time: 1:58)

Director Richard Fleischer and ace British cinematographer Jack Cardiff perched their cameras atop a seven hundred year old seaside castle in Dinard, France, to capture this exquisitely scenic swordfight in the sky. Blood-feuding half-brothers Einar (Kirk Dougas) and Eric (Tony Curtis) cross tenth century swords all over a steeply-graded tower like war-eagles battling over a nest of stone. (See *The Vikings*, pages 88–89.)

Scaramouche (1952) (Screen time: 5:38)

The longest duel in screen history (French Revolution-era half-brothers) has been clocked as high as ten minutes in duration by proud pair-ent Stewart Granger (in his book *Sparks Fly Upward*), but five and a half is more the mark. It took three fencers to complete this fluid and acrobatic MGM martial arts production number staged in, above, and through the elaborate set for the 18th century Theatre Ambigu: Granger (as Andre Moreau/Scaramouche), fellow star Mel Ferrer (as dueling-crazed Noel, Marquis de Maynes) and European fencing champion Jean Heremans (who doubles quite seamlessly for Ferrer in certain over-the-shoulder and long shots). (See *Scaramouche*, pages 66–69.)

Tony Curtis, Kirk Douglas (1958 lobby card)

CORNERED . . . Stewart Granger holds Mel Ferrer at swords point, determined to avenge the death of his friend.

M·G·M's *Scaramouche* Color by TECHNICOLOR

Mel Ferrer, Stewart Granger (1952 photo lobby card)

MONTGOMERY CLIFT · ELIZABETH TAYLOR · EVA MARIE SAINT

M·G·M PRESENTS IN M·G·M CAMERA 65 "WINDOW OF THE WORLD"

RAINTREE COUNTY

IN THE GREAT TRADITION OF CIVIL WAR ROMANCE

co-starring
NIGEL PATRICK · LEE MARVIN with **ROD TAYLOR · AGNES MOOREHEAD**
WALTER ABEL · JARMA LEWIS · TOM DRAKE · Screen Play by **MILLARD KAUFMAN** Associate Producer

Based on the Novel by Ross Lockridge, Jr. · Print by TECHNICOLOR® · Directed by **EDWARD DMYTRYK** · Produced by **DAVID LEWIS**   AN M·G·M PICTURE

Title card (1957)

THE MOVIES & THE POSTERS
(1932-1970)

THE SIGN OF THE CROSS

(PARAMOUNT — 1932)

CAST: Fredric March, Elissa Landi, Claudette Colbert,
Charles Laughton, Ian Keith
PRODUCER/DIRECTOR: Cecil B. DeMille
SCREENPLAY: Waldemar Young and Sidney Buchman;
based on the play by Wilson Barrett
MUSIC: Rudolph Kopp
DIRECTOR OF PHOTOGRAPHY: Karl Struss
140 minutes / black and white

Daybill (1940s)

While Cecil DeMille had mastered the epic production possibilities of silent on-location filmmaking with *The Ten Commandments* (1923) and *The King of Kings* (1927), talking pictures actually cramped his scope. Due to the awkward production technicalities of early sound filmmaking and Paramount's ongoing desire to peer over his financial shoulder, DeMille resorted to the Paramount backlot and ranch to create this and most of his subsequent historical spectacles.

For better and worse, then, DeMille's sound era epic production style is established *en bloc* in his first effort, *The Sign of the Cross*, which was shot in eight weeks for $650,000. All the elements for which his work has been praised and pilloried are present here: lavish Art Deco-influenced sets and costumes, a paternalistic attitude toward the audience and the subject matter, a tin ear for the writing and acting of period dialogue, an over-reliance on authenticity-straining backlot production techniques.

64 A.D. Emperor Nero (37–68) (a daring Hollywood debut by a young, fleshy, false-Roman-nosed DeMille discovery named Charles Laughton) has just sung and sulked his way through the third night of the great fire which decimates much of Rome. With the citizenry incensed at the apathy of the sexually free-ranging emperor and his similarly-inclined wife, Poppaea (Claudette Colbert), Nero and ambitious aide, Tigellinus (Ian Keith) conspire to blame the fire on the ever-increasing Christians. This puts a terminal crimp in the dating profile of swinging-prefect-about-town, Marcus Superbus (Fredric March, a fashion victim for the ages in gilded chain mail), who bypasses Poppaea and follows Christian beauty Mercia (Elissa Landi) to the lions in the name of love.

Apart from Laughton's bold turn and some memorable set pieces (Poppaea's bath in the milk of asses, the sundry forms of martyrdom in the arena), the gratingly inapt early 1930's attitudes and speaking voices of many of the players seriously date the film. Movie paper on this title is rare and pricey (One-sheet: $800). The stone lithograph daybill depicted was undoubtedly produced for a post-World War II reissue of the film.

Ian Keith, Elissa Landi, Fredric March (1944 reissue lobby card)

CLEOPATRA

(PARAMOUNT — 1934)

CAST: Claudette Colbert, Warren William, Henry Wilcoxon,
Joseph Schildkraut, Ian Keith, Gertrude Michael, C. Aubrey Smith
PRODUCER/DIRECTOR: Cecil B. DeMille
SCREENPLAY: Waldemar Young and Vincent Lawrence
MUSIC: Rudolph Kopp
DIRECTOR OF PHOTOGRAPHY: Victor Milner
101 minutes / black and white

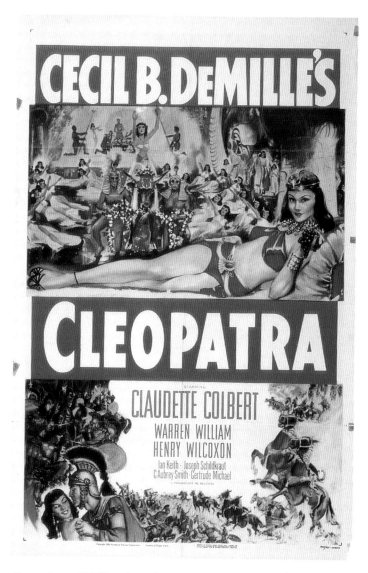

One-sheet (1952 reissue)

In the catalogue *Hollywood and History: Costume Design In Film,* curator Edward Maeder makes the crucial distinction between *accuracy* and *anachronism* in period film costume design: *". . . (A)nachronisms are found in almost every motion picture that portrays another period. While presenting an illusion of an earlier time, these movies rarely replicate the exact look that prevailed; instead the costumes take elements from past styles and combine them with aspects of contemporary fashion."*

This premise can be blown out to apply to the overall production design of Cecil B. DeMille's 1934 version of *Cleopatra,* which could've been subtitled: *The Art Deco Splendor That Was Ancient Egypt and Rome.* DeMille refuted critics of his custom blend of the historically accurate and contemporarily chic with the credo: *Audiences do not want to be educated, but entertained.* As much a silent film as a sound one (no prints exist of "vamp" Theda Bara's 1917 silent effort), the film's pleasures, big and small, derive far more from what is seen than what is spoken: kitschy Deco-gyptian main titles; Cleopatra's outrageously elaborate barge; a glitzy toga party with sea weed-wrapped women on the half shell and an all-female "orchestra" 48 B.C.-style.

Storywise, Cleopatra, Queen of Egypt (69–30 B.C.), (Claudette Colbert) employs her guile to stave off total Roman domination as exercised by serial lovers Julius Caesar (100–44 B.C.) (Warren William) and Marc Antony (83–30 B.C.) (Henry Wilcoxon). Unfortunately, it all plays like an over-produced chapter of Universal's *Flash Gordon* serial, only worse. Colbert is a 1930s screen personality whose allure flags badly today, the same, in spades, for William and Wilcoxon. Watch it with the sound off.

Fortunately, the visual style of the film transfers to the imagery of the original poster and promotional art. (Note trade ad detail on page 39.) Auction prices for Cleopatra's Art Deco-rated paper items are regal: one-sheet ($6,300); jumbo lobby card set ($3,200); window card ($1,500).

Trade ad detail (1934)

CLEOPATRA AND MARC ANTONY

Claudette Colbert and Henry Wilcoxon in " Cleopatra."

(Paramount)

Silver plate photo (1934)

THE LIVES OF A BENGAL LANCER

(PARAMOUNT — 1935)

CAST: Gary Cooper, Franchot Tone, Richard Cromwell,
Sir Guy Standing, C. Aubrey Smith, Monte Blue, Kathleen Burke,
Akim Tamiroff
PRODUCER: Louis Lighton
DIRECTOR: Henry Hathaway
SCREENPLAY: Waldemar Young, John L. Balderston and
Achmed Abdullah; based on the book by Major Francis Yeats-Brown;
adapted by Grover Jones and William Slavens McNutt
MUSIC: Milan Roder
DIRECTOR OF PHOTOGRAPHY: Charles Lang
109 minutes / black and white

One-sheet (1950 reissue—unrestored)

If *The Lives of a Bengal Lancer* plays like a lexicon of every British empire/French Foreign Legion adventure cliche in the book, that's because it is. The unexpected box office success of the film is the true wellspring for the succession of similar epics which paraded out of Hollywood and Great Britain over the next four decades: *The Charge of the Light Brigade* (1936); *Under Two Flags* (1936); *Drums* (1938); *Gunga Din* (1939); *Beau Geste* (1939); *The Four Feathers* (1939); *The Light that Failed* (1940); *King of the Khyber Rifles* (1953); *Flame Over India* (1960); *Zulu* (1964); *Khartoum* (1966); *The Man Who Would Be King* (1976). The film was also nominated for Best Picture and Best Director Academy Awards.

This seminal *buddy picture* unites very American Gary Cooper, Franchot Tone, and Richard Cromwell as 41st Regiment officers itching for open battle against the tribal forces of the urbane, Oxford-educated chieftain, Mohammed Khan (Douglas Dumbrille). Cooper's the carper, Tone cracks wise, and Cromwell's the crybaby. Upholding the regimental traditions and the British accents are Sir Guy Standing as Cromwell's commanding officer (first) and estranged father (second) and C. Aubrey Smith as his aide. After assorted skirmishes, the trio's dreams of glory evaporate when they become surprise after-dinner hostages in the Khan's palace and are tortured for information by their versatile host himself.

Except for a spectacular pitched battle finale (which earned a now-defunct Oscar category Best Assistant Director Academy Award), this trim period production boasts authentic costumes and sets and atmospheric black and white cinematography dripping with 1930s exoticism. Director Henry Hathaway selected locations near California's Sierra Nevada Range to double for India's mountainous frontier. Despite the ultra-scarcity of original release paper from the film, little value is attached to the 1950 reissue items pictured here.

with
GARY COOPER

FRANCHOT
TONE

RICHARD
CROMWELL

SIR GUY
STANDING

C. AUBREY SMITH

MONTE BLUE

KATHLEEN BURKE

Directed by HENRY HATHAWAY

From the Novel by Francis Yeats-Brown

A PARAMOUNT CHAMPION Brought Back By Popular Demand

The LiVES OF A BENGAL LANCER

Kathleen Burke, Gary Cooper (1950 reissue lobby card)

THE CRUSADES

(PARAMOUNT — 1935)

CAST: Loretta Young, Henry Wilcoxon, Ian Keith, C. Aubrey Smith, Katherine DeMille, Joseph Schildkraut, Alan Hale, C. Henry Gordon
PRODUCER/DIRECTOR: Cecil B. DeMille
SCREENPLAY: Harold Lamb, Waldemar Young, and Dudley Nichols; based on Lamb's book *The Crusades: Iron Men and Saints*
MUSIC: Rudolph Kopp
DIRECTOR OF PHOTOGRAPHY: Victor Milner
123 minutes / black and white

One-sheet (1948 reissue)

In the Third Crusade (1189–1192), Richard the Lionhearted, King of England (1157–1199), and his combined European forces fought Salah al-Din Yusuf ibn-Ayyud (Saladin) (1137–1193) and his Saracens to a standoff which resulted in a negotiated settlement over access to the Holy City of Jerusalem. Cecil B. DeMille's attempt to re-take the Holy Land for Hollywood with *The Crusades* is far less successful.

In the book *The Hollywood History of the World*, George MacDonald Fraser calls *The Crusades* ". . . DeMille at his worst, a confused romantic mess of a film ostensibly trying to condense into two hours the essence of a chapter of human history which lasted two centuries and shaped the future of Europe—DeMille called it 'telescoping history.'" The story assembles the correct additional historical personages for the undertaking: Peter the Hermit; Frederick I, Barbarossa, of Germany; Phillip II, Augustus, of France, etc. Unfortunately, it then embroils them in talky war councils and intrigues which are relieved by two major action set pieces: the nighttime storming of the walls of the city of Acre and a frenetic head-on clash of armored horse.

Glopped on top of this medieval melange is a whopper of a love triangle (sorry, C.B.) involving Richard (Henry Wilcoxon), his hastily-arranged bride, Berengaria of Navarre (Loretta Young) and Salah al-Din himself (Ian Keith). The lackluster response to *The Crusades* resulted in DeMille's turning to more familiar American themes for all but two of his remaining features: *The Plainsman* (1937); *The Buccaneer* (1938); *Union Pacific* (1939); *North West Mounted Police* (1940); *Reap the Wild Wind* (1942); *The Story of Dr. Wassell* (1944); *Unconquered* (1947); *The Greatest Show on Earth* (1952).

The original movie poster art from the film is handsome and costly (one-sheet: $600). Paramount re-released the film in 1948 to capitalize on Young's Best Actress Academy Award the year before for *The Farmer's Daughter*. This accounts for the layout of the fiery Morgan Lithograph 1948 reissue one-sheet depicted on this page (Value: $200).

Katherine DeMille, Henry Wilcoxon, Loretta Young (1935 lobby card—censorship stamp)

THE LAST DAYS OF POMPEII

(RKO — 1935)

CAST: Preston Foster, Alan Hale, Basil Rathbone, John Wood,
Louis Calhern, David Holt, Dorothy Wilson
PRODUCER: Merian C. Cooper
DIRECTOR: Ernest B. Schoedsack
SCREENPLAY: Ruth Rose and Boris Ingster
MUSIC: Roy Webb
DIRECTOR OF PHOTOGRAPHY: J. Roy Hunt
SPECIAL VISUAL EFFECTS: Willis O'Brien
100 minutes / black and white

Theater lobby standee (1935)

The concept of the last days of the ancient Roman city of Pompeii and its destruction in 79 A.D. by the eruption of Mount Vesuvius panders to the earliest "show and see" sensationalism of the nickelodeon era. Given its local setting, pioneering Italian silent filmmakers couldn't wait to get their sprockets on Edward Bulwer-Lytton's (1803–1873) 1834 literary chestnut, *The Last Days of Pompeii*, for story matter to scatter amongst the volcanic debris; three competing abbreviated silent versions were produced there in 1913 alone. Subsequent *Pompeii*'s include a 1926 Italian silent directed by Carmine Gallone and the 1960 Steve Reeves vehicle pictured on page 139.

An opening title for RKO's 1935 spectacle forswears any relation to Bulwer-Lytton's novel, leaving the blame for this dunderheaded effort squarely at the feet of the filmmakers. Like its campy sister, RKO fantasy spectacle *She* (see pages 6–7), which had been released earlier that year, *The Last Days of Pompeii* offers some pomp with no compelling story circumstances. True, producer Merian C. Cooper had co-written-produced-directed *King Kong* with Ernest Schoedsack for RKO in 1933, but neither *She* nor *The Last Days of Pompeii* could hold a banana to it in either concept or execution.

This swords-to-riches spectacle features a one thousand percent miscast Preston Foster as a Wallace Beery-sounding ancient blacksmith driven to turn gladiator. The dialogue and accents are pure Iowa corn and the arena action is surprisingly brief and unexceptional. *King Kong* special effects pioneer Willis O'Brien created a huge Colossus of Rhodes-style stone gladiator which topples spectacularly in the volcanic finale.

Critical brickbats aside, *The Last Days of Pompeii* was accorded full blockbuster status by RKO, which issued an oversized pressbook with elaborate color covers to hype the pyrotechnics. For that reason, the pressbook detail on page 45 offers a rare opportunity to see the full range of poster styles depicted in color. The seldom-seen *Pompeii* one-sheet auctions for as high as $700.

24 SHEET

MELODRAMATIC SELLING PAPER
BUILT FOR ACE SHOWMANSHIP

6 SHEET

3 SHEET / 1 SHEET

EXCEPTIONAL power predominates in all this full-color lithographed billboard and display material, affording an attendance compelling campaign fully up to the high audience appeal of the show.

Order direct from

RKO RADIO Exchanges

MINIATURE WINDOW CARD / WINDOW CARD / JUMBO WINDOW CARD

BURGEE MULTICOLOR GOLD FRINGED EACH 65c

TIRE COVER EACH 60c

40x60 BOTH GORGEOUSLY COLORED EACH $1.50 . . . . PAIR $2.50

Pressbook detail (1935)

45

CAPTAIN BLOOD

(WARNER BROS. — 1935)

CAST: Errol Flynn, Olivia de Havilland, Lionel Atwill, Basil Rathbone, Henry Stephenson
PRODUCER: Hal B. Wallis
DIRECTOR: Michael Curtiz
SCREENPLAY: Casey Robinson; based on the novel by Rafael Sabatini
MUSIC: Erich Wolfgang Korngold
DIRECTOR OF PHOTOGRAPHY: Hal Mohr
119 minutes / black and white

Daybill (1940s)

When British star Robert Donat (*The Count of Monte Cristo*—1934) bowed out of the title role of Warner Brothers' remake of *Captain Blood* (J. Warren Kerrigan starred in the 1924 silent), he created an opportunity for an obscure Warner's contract player to become the sound era successor to the genre's still well-remembered silent era creator and biggest star, Douglas Fairbanks. The player: Errol Leslie Thomson Flynn. The result: a Best Picture Academy Award nomination for the film and instant international stardom for Flynn.

The witty, agile, courageous archetype which Flynn embodied seemed to inhabit characters from across the centuries with a charm and naturalness which left one wondering where history tapered off and Flynn began. Here was the seeming authenticity of personality, romance, and swordsmanship which DeMille's protagonists glaringly lacked—a living special effect so potent on screen and at the box office that mogul Jack Warner, whom Flynn often despised, poured tens of millions of dollars into an armada of Flynn adventure vehicles for the next eighteen years.

At his peak, this Australian-born screen legend almost outshone the collective talents of the contract stock company surrounding him in the examples pictured here: producer Hal Wallis, director Michael Curtiz, composer Erich Wolfgang Korngold, eight-time leading lady Olivia de Havilland, perennial sidekick Alan Hale, seminal screen villains Basil Rathbone and Claude Rains, etc.

These four pages illustrate Flynn's finest swordfighting heroes: the foppish doctor-turned-privateer, Peter Blood; the beguiling screen Robin Hood all others are measured by; Geoffrey Thorpe of *The Sea Hawk*, to this day the finest pirate adventure Hollywood has been able to launch. Movie poster art from top Flynn titles like these command major auction prices (The best to date: *Robin Hood* 3-sheet—$19,550.) The *Captain Blood* and *Robin Hood* Australian daybills are reproduced here for the first time anywhere. (See *Errol Flynn: The Movie Posters* for further information.)

Olivia de Havilland, Errol Flynn (1935 lobby card)

Daybill (1940s)

Errol Flynn, Basil Rathbone

Olivia de Havilland, Errol Flynn

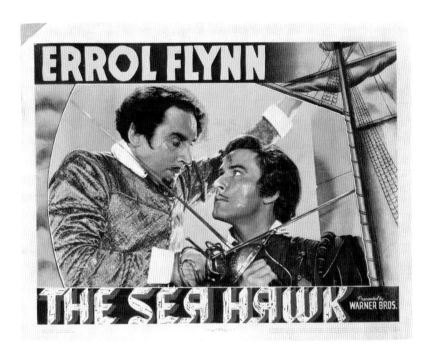

Henry Daniell, Errol Flynn

Brenda Marshall, Errol Flynn

Belgian poster (1940s)

NORTHWEST PASSAGE

(METRO-GOLDWYN-MAYER — 1940)

CAST: Spencer Tracy, Robert Young, Walter Brennan, Ruth Hussey, Nat Pendleton, Isabel Jewell
PRODUCER: Hunt Stromberg
DIRECTOR: King Vidor
SCREENPLAY: Laurence Stallings and Talbot Jennings; based on the novel by Kenneth Roberts
MUSIC: Herbert Stothart
DIRECTORS OF PHOTOGRAPHY: Sidney Wagner and William V. Skall
125 minutes / Technicolor

One-sheet (1940—Style D—on linen)

Northwest Passage is an impressively executed and photographed Technicolor frontier epic with unsettling undertones. Based on the first half of Kenneth Roberts' (1885–1957) 1937 novel of the same title, the film depicts the harrowing exploits of Colonel Robert Rogers of Connecticut (1717–1795). Roberts organized a crack British-Colonial (American) militia battalion, "Rogers' Rangers," and attached them to the British Army during the French and Indian War (1756–1763). In 1759, he led his two hundred men on an agonizing round-trip trek through enemy country to St. Francis, Canada. Here, they annihilated the main encampment of the Abenaki Indians who had amassed hundreds of scalps in carrying out a lengthy backwoods war on settlements south of the Canadian border.

Director King Vidor seems to have spared his cast, led by Spencer Tracy as Roberts, few of the hardships experienced by the real Rangers. This extraordinarily physical production features a series of complex and arduous action set pieces shot near Lake Payette, Idaho. One involves the portage of leaden whale boats up, then slowly down, a steep headland to avoid detection by their adversaries. The other depicts the remarkable on-camera creation of a human chain to ford a raging river.

In justifying what was essentially the near-massacre of the Abenakis, the screenplay repeatedly and graphically recounts Abenaki barbarism and positions an immense pole of dangling scalps in our face during and after the St. Francis raid. Was this an allegory about the all-out ruthlessness which would be required to win the already-raging World War II? Out of that context, today's audiences could find Roberts' smug savagery a touch genocidal, especially when he renames an orphaned Abenaki "Billy" as the boy stares back at the smoking remains of his village.

The handsome likeness of Tracy on the one-sheet depicted on this page is a typical example of MGM's in-house poster style: finely detailed star portraiture against a white background. Value: $400–600.

Title card (1940)

CAPTAIN FROM CASTILE

(TWENTIETH CENTURY-FOX — 1947)

CAST: Tyrone Power, Jean Peters, Cesar Romero, Lee J. Cobb,
John Sutton, Antonio Moreno, Thomas Gomez, Alan Mowbray,
Barbara Lawrence, Marc Lawrence
PRODUCER: Lamarr Trotti
DIRECTOR: Henry King
SCREENPLAY: Lamarr Trotti; based on the novel by Samuel Shellabarger
MUSIC: Alfred Newman
DIRECTORS OF PHOTOGRAPHY: Charles Clarke and Arthur E. Arling
140 minutes / Technicolor

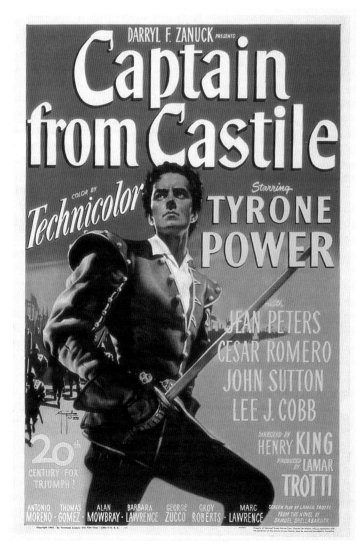

One-sheet (1947—restored on linen—art by Gargiulo)

While the costume vehicles tailored for his nearest rival, Errol Flynn, were as flippant as the man himself, Tyrone Power projected a heroic earnestness into his body of work in the cycle which entitles him to a share of Flynn's crown as the reigning romantic adventure star of the later 1930s through the late 1940s. After World War II, Fox mogul Darryl F. Zanuck repeatedly sent contract star Power and a Hollywood contingent to overseas locations to film screenplay versions of period romantic novels. Samuel Shellabarger's (1888–1954) 1945 work, *Captain from Castile*, which concerns aristocratic Pedro De Vargas' flight from the Spanish Inquisition and subsequent adventures in Mexico with Hernando Cortez' 1518 expedition, garnered the most elaborate treatment.

Shot on locations around Mexico (which also doubled for Spain), the film is a beautifully muted masterwork undone by a long, anti-climactic aftermath to its dark and spellbinding opening. In this brisk, novella-like portion, the horror of persecution by the Inquisition is brought to full boil. Pedro (Power) and family are unjustly imprisoned—and his young sister tortured to death—by the liquidly evil minion Diego De Silva (John Sutton). The bittersweetness is modulated by composer Alfred Newman's most haunting romantic score and by the stunning screen debut of a luscious Jean Peters as the hopelessly smitten peasant girl, Catana. Once the story shifts to Mexico, the blazing opening story embers die. The painterly Gargiulo one-sheet on this page usually fetches $400–500 at auction.

Far more satisfying literarily is the cunning epic screenwriter Milton Krims cleaved out of Shellabarger's next, *Prince of Foxes* (1947). Power portrays fifteenth century Italian artist and rogue Andre Orsini. His delicately nefarious undertakings for Count Cesare Borgia (Orson Welles in top form) render this rich-looking black and white pageant a true *epique noir*. Lastly, Thomas B. Costain's (1885–1965) 13th century England and Cathay-set novel, *The Black Rose* (1945) suffers the same structural fate as *Captain from Castile* without its excitement or that of its own one-sheet pictured on page 54.

Inside the photo:

DARRYL F. ZANUCK present

Captain from Castile

starring

TYRONE POWER

COLOR BY *TECHNICOLOR*

with JEAN PETERS · CESAR ROMERO · JOHN SUTTON · LEE J. COBB

20th CENTURY-FOX

Directed by HENRY KING   Produced by LAMAR TROTTI

John Sutton, Antonio Moreno, Tyrone Power (1947 lobby card)

53

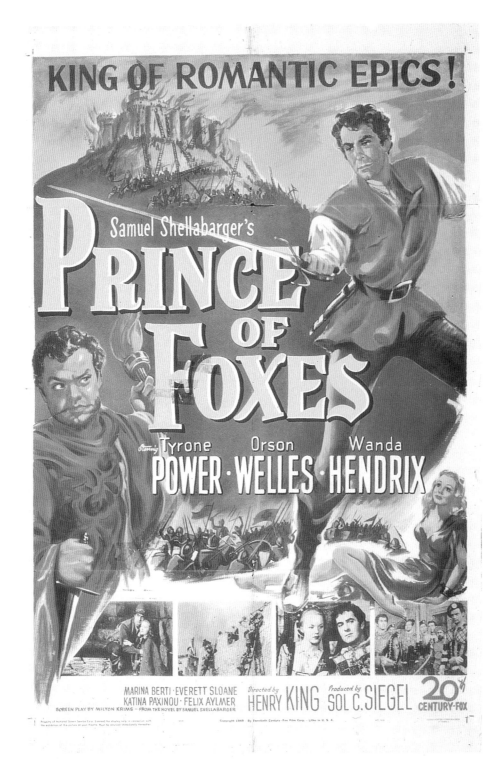

One-sheet (1949)

Tyrone Power, Orson Welles

Everett Sloane, Tyrone Power

Tyrone Power, Orson Welles, Jack Hawkins

Cecile Aubrey, Tyrone Power, Jack Hawkins

One-sheet (1950)

SAMSON AND DELILAH

(PARAMOUNT — 1949)

CAST: Hedy Lamarr, Victor Mature, George Sanders,
Angela Lansbury, Henry Wilcoxon
PRODUCER/DIRECTOR: Cecil B. DeMille
SCREENPLAY: Jesse L. Lasky, Jr. and Fredric M. Frank
MUSIC: Victor Young
DIRECTOR OF PHOTOGRAPHY: George Barnes
131 minutes / Technicolor

One-sheet (1949—restored on linen)

Cecil B. DeMille's first Technicolor Biblical spectacle, *Samson and Delilah*, was one of the most popular entertainments of the day, its mighty $11 million in 1950 box office rentals briefly surpassing those of *Gone With the Wind*. Compared to the tautness of *Captain from Castile* and *Prince of Foxes*, *Samson and Delilah* is flabby hokum, but its great success stimulated the Hollywood costume blockbuster revival of the 1950s. Still, DeMille's stylistic slippage is showing badly in this garishly colorful backlot spectacle which was repeatedly re-released throughout the 1950s and 1960s. In fact, the two 1959 reissue posters on page 58 were designed to capitalize on the then-raging success of Steve Reeves' similarly muscular *Hercules*. (See pages 134–149.)

A cast of dozens is more often the case in this retelling of the Biblical tale of super strong Samson, the Judge of Dan (Victor Mature), and the all-empowering dark hair and wandering-eyes-for-Philistine-women which he loses to the sensual treachery of the jealous Delilah (Hedy Lamarr). Neither star was DeMille's first choice. For a post-MGM Lamarr, it was a last glamorous hurrah, while Mature churned out costume spectacles for the next decade. Lamarr and a golden delicious young Angela Lansbury, as her ill-fated sister, Semadar, get the best out of the five credited costume designers; most of the Philistine males, like George Sanders and Henry Wilcoxon, sport gilded, vanity-size trash can-style helmets for Samson to bash in with whatever or whomever is handy.

The staging of many of the Biblical acts of strength performed by Mature's un-toned Samson has staled as well, especially his tussle with the stuffed stand-in depicted on page 57. The film's most hallowed set piece, the blinded Samson's toppling of the temple of Dagon, was actually a meticulously-assembled final composite matte shot which "stacked" the levels of live action vertically in the frame. It's still a good show.

The colorful one-sheet on this page has auctioned as high as $2,000, but its more realistic value is $400–600.

CECIL B. DeMILLE'S MASTERPIECE **Samson and Delilah**

COLOR BY
TECHNICOLOR

Starring

**HEDY
LAMARR**

**VICTOR
MATURE**

**GEORGE
SANDERS**

**ANGELA
LANSBURY**

**HENRY
WILCOXON**

Produced and Directed by
CECIL B. DeMILLE

Screenplay by Jesse L. Lasky, Jr. Fredric M. Frank
From original treatments by
Harold Lamb & Vladimir Jabotinsky
Based upon the history of Samson & Delilah
in the Holy Bible. Judges 13-16
A PARAMOUNT PICTURE

Copyright 1949 Paramount Pictures Inc. Country of origin U.S.A.   4   Property of National Screen Service Corp. Licensed for display only in connection with the exhibition of this picture at your theatre. Must be returned immediately thereafter.   49/654

Victor Mature (1949 lobby card)

One-sheet (1959 reissue—unrestored)

Daybill (1959 reissue)

Souvenir program detail (1949)

DAVID AND BATHSHEBA

(TWENTIETH CENTURY-FOX — 1951)

CAST: Gregory Peck, Susan Hayward, Raymond Massey,
Kieron Moore, James Robertson Justice, Jane Meadows,
John Sutton, Francis X. Bushman, Walter Talun
PRODUCER: Darryl F. Zanuck
DIRECTOR: Henry King
SCREENPLAY: Phillip Dunne
MUSIC: Alfred Newman
DIRECTOR OF PHOTOGRAPHY: Lee Garmes
116 minutes / Technicolor

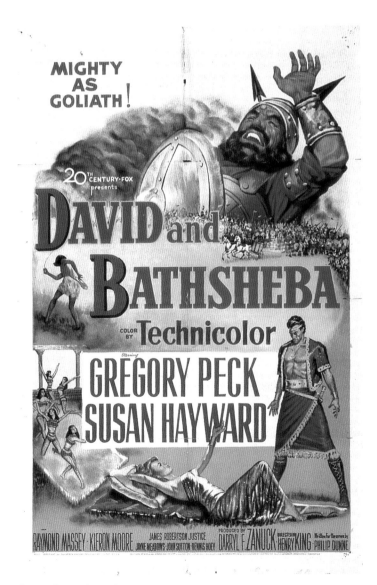

One-sheet (1951)

David and Bathsheba is one of the most satisfying and literate Biblical epics depicted in this study. It is also a rich reminder of the 1940's Fox Technicolor production style which would soon be mutated by the studio's retooling for Cinemascope in 1953. The screenplay by longtime Fox screenwriter-producer-director Philip Dunne is based on the *Second Book of Samuel* in the *Old Testament*. It dramatizes the controversial relationship between David, King of Israel (1040?–970? B.C.), portrayed by a surging Gregory Peck, and the sensuous Bathsheba, the soldier's wife David covets (Susan Hayward).

Dunne's multi-faceted exploration of David's character is the key to the film's quality. Harried by a pesky war with the Ammonites, the self-righteous hectoring of the prophet Nathan (Raymond Massey) and take-no-emotional-prisoners encounters with estranged first wife Michal (Jayne Meadows), David is a joyless, isolated figure. Pacing the terrace of his palace one sleepless night, he spies Bathsheba bathing on an adjacent roof. David later summons her and learns that she is the all-but-in-name-only spouse of one his most dedicated front line soldiers, Uriah the Hittite (Kieron Moore).

And, ultimately, it's to the front line where Uriah is dispatched in an immoral and desperate hope his death will legitimize the child Bathsheba soon carries for David. Dunne's screenplay clings tenaciously to David's psyche throughout the spiritual turmoil, including a riveting flashback to David's boyhood encounter with Goliath (played by professional wrestler Walter "The Polish Angel" Talun). Once more, composer Alfred Newman contributes an exquisitely-regal and bittersweet series of musical themes. Not surprisingly, *David and Bathsheba* captured $7 million in rentals as the number one grossing film of 1951. Like *Samson and Delilah*, the film was given a Biblical muscleman ad campaign makeover and reissued in 1960 to capitalize on the success of *Hercules* the prior year. (See pages 134–149.)

Title card (1951—unrestored)

THE RED BADGE OF COURAGE

(METRO-GOLDWYN-MAYER — 1951)

CAST: Audie Murphy, Bill Mauldin, Douglas Dick, Royal Dano, John Dierkes, Arthur Hunnicutt, Andy Devine, Robert Easton, Smith Ballew, Glenn Strange
PRODUCER: Gottfried Reinhardt
DIRECTOR: John Huston
SCREENPLAY: John Huston; based on the novel by Stephen Crane; adapted by Albert Band
MUSIC: Bronislau Kaper
DIRECTOR OF PHOTOGRAPHY: Harold Rosson
69 minutes / black and white

This extraordinary adaptation of Stephen Crane's (1871–1900) 1895 Civil War literary classic has always existed more as a footnote than as a milestone in the careers of both filmmaker John Huston and actor Audie Murphy. That's probably because Metro-Goldwyn-Mayer gave Huston and producer Gottfried Reinhardt an eyebrow-raising $1.6 million budget to film this poetic black and white masterwork —and then excised an eyebrow-raising nine minutes in distributing it to oblivion as a second feature.

Stylistically, *The Red Badge of Courage* is unlike any of Huston's films or any of the formal historical epics which preceded it. Huston took his black and white film stock and no-name cast out into the fields and forests and created a daringly lyrical, woodsy feature length set piece. To focus the story ever closely on the ensemble company of "green" Union infantry played by Audie Murphy, Bill Mauldin, and others, Huston swarmed his masses of Union and Confederate infantry and cavalry deep in the frame.

Coltish World War II hero Murphy (24 citations including the Congressional Medal of Honor) had not yet settled into the bland series of 1950s and 1960s program westerns which would serve as his screen legacy. Huston embraced the baby-faced vulnerability which Murphy's other directors grappled to conceal and poured it down the barrel of the lens. For probably the only time in his fifty-plus film career, Murphy didn't have to try to act. All the fear, false bravado, and tenderness of Henry Fleming pour unbidden from Murphy's Texas moon-shaped face. Here is the real-life hero playing a coward, knowing full well that the difference between being one or the other is immeasurable. Murphy's wide open performance is a resonant slice of motion picture Americana. Perhaps then, *The Red Badge of Courage* is the most appropriate epitaph for a star-crossed hero who never really returned from the war that made him world famous. Now, that's epic.

Poster art from *The Red Badge of Courage* is scarce but nominally priced (One-sheet: $100). The lobby card on page 63 was printed slightly out of color registration.

Belgian poster (1952—trimmed)

Audie Murphy, Bill Mauldin, John Dierkes (1951 lobby card)

QUO VADIS

(METRO-GOLDWYN-MAYER — 1951)

CAST: Robert Taylor, Deborah Kerr, Leo Genn, Peter Ustinov, Patricia Laffan, Finlay Currie, Abraham Sofaer, Marina Berti, Buddy Baer, Felix Aylmer, Nora Swinburne
PRODUCER: Sam Zimbalist
DIRECTOR: Mervyn LeRoy
SCREENPLAY: John Lee Mahin, S.N. Behrman, and Sonya Levien; based on the novel by Henryk Sienkiewicz
MUSIC: Miklos Rozsa
DIRECTORS OF PHOTOGRAPHY: Robert Surtees and William V. Skall
171 minutes / Technicolor

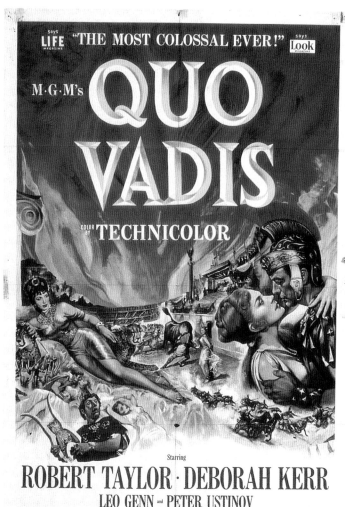

One-sheet (1951—tape stains)

Metro-Goldwyn-Mayer dramatically upped the ante in the historical epic sweepstakes when they committed a then-stratospheric $7 million budget to see how much extra production value they could fluke by shooting *Quo Vadis* in lire, and English, at Cinecitta Studios in Rome. Director Mervyn LeRoy and a picked Hollywood crew worked with armies of Italian technicians, artisans, and extras to mount first century Roman spectacles of an unprecedented scale; a triumphal procession in front of Nero's palace; sections of the Circus Maximus large enough to seat 6,000 carefully platooned extras; four flaming blocks of period buildings for Nero's burning of Rome. The gamble paid off handsomely: $10.5 million in U.S. box office rentals alone and three 1951 Academy Award nominations, including Best Picture.

The characters are basically identical to DeMille's 1932 *The Sign of the Cross*: Emperor Nero (a young Peter Ustinov, acting up a storm), swinging wife Popaea (Patricia Laffan), hale and hedonistic conquering commander Marcus Vinicius (Robert Taylor), and angelic Christian beauty, Lygia (Deborah Kerr), who'd rather sit in a lion's mouth than on Marcus' lap. A very entertaining dress rehearsal for *Ben-Hur* eight years hence, *Quo Vadis* is a truly large and lavish spectacle bolstered by excellent performances by Kerr, Ustinov, and Leo Genn (the latter two receiving Best Supporting Actor Academy Award nominations).

The studio gambled on declining contract star Taylor, and his Nebraska accent, to carry the picture after first choice Stewart Granger refused to sign a studio contract to do the film. Taylor is utterly miscast as the arrogant pagan who comes to Christ, but the success of the film guaranteed his very American presence in Leo the Lion's upcoming raft of medieval pageants (see *Ivanhoe*, page 70). The everything-but-the-kitchen-sink artwork depicted on the one-sheet on this page and the title card back on page 22 define the style of the epic Hollywood sell.

Half sheet (1951—style B—unrestored—censorship sticker)

SCARAMOUCHE

(METRO-GOLDWYN-MAYER — 1952)

CAST: Stewart Granger, Eleanor Parker, Janet Leigh, Mel Ferrer,
Henry Wilcoxon, Nina Foch, Lewis Stone, Richard Anderson
PRODUCER: Carey Wilson
DIRECTOR: George Sidney
SCREENPLAY: Ronald Millar and George Froeschel; based on the novel
by Rafael Sabatini
MUSIC: Victor Young
DIRECTOR OF PHOTOGRAPHY: Charles Rosher
118 minutes / Technicolor

One-sheet (1952)

After establishing himself in a series of ornate British period films *(The Man in Grey, Saraband)*, swashbuckling Stewart Granger got his crack at the title role—and the title of Hollywood's leading 1950s screen swordsman—in Metro-Goldwyn-Mayer's sumptuous Technicolor remake of Rafael Sabatini's (1875–1950) 1921 novel, *Scaramouche*. (Ramon Novarro and Lewis Stone starred in the studio's 1925 silent.) Granger's most memorable and spectacular role, *Scaramouche* is also one of the last truly elaborate 18th century-set spectacles to be mounted in Hollywood proper.

A French Revolution-era tale of revenge and illegitimacy, *Scaramouche* concerns handsome, witty, petticoat-chasing Andre Moreau (Granger), whose sudden desire to discover the identity of his lifelong benefactor leads him to run afoul of the cold-blooded steel wielded by famed duelist, Noel, Marquis de Maynes (Mel Ferrer). (See *Trial by Combat* on page 37 for a description of *Scaramouche*'s marathon fencing finale.) In the process, Andre becomes a fugitive, taking refuge in a minstrel company as the clown "Scaramouche" until he can hone his dueling skills to take on de Maynes. Director George Sidney's recreations of the theatrical productions of the period are among the delights of the film, as are Eleanor Parker as Andre's saucy lover, Lenore, and Janet Leigh as the ingenuous Aline de Gavrilac.

A latter day studio style triumph, *Scaramouche* accomplished its ornate production design through the construction of elaborate recreations of portions of Marie Antoinette's (Nina Foch) chambers at Versailles and the multi-story Theatre Ambigu. Portions of Golden Gate Park in San Francisco double for the lush French countryside depicted in the opening. The one-sheet illustrated on this page is another example of the studio's heavy-on-the-white-background movie poster style. (Value: $100–150.) The autograph reads: *"For my new friend, Lawrence. We'll go on collecting. All the best, Stewart Granger"*. (Ed. note: The author and the late Mr. Granger traded movie posters in the early 1990s.)

Title card (1952)

Mel Ferrer, Stewart Granger

Eleanor Parker, Stewart Granger

Eleanor Parker, Janet Leigh

Mel Ferrer, Stewart Granger

RAFAEL SABATINI'S

SCARAMOUCHE

M-G-M's *Spectacular* COLOR BY TECHNICOLOR MASTERPIECE!

STARRING

STEWART GRANGER
ELEANOR PARKER
JANET LEIGH
MEL FERRER

with **HENRY WILCOXON · NINA FOCH · LEWIS STONE · RICHARD ANDERSON**

Screen Play by **RONALD MILLAR** and **GEORGE FROESCHEL** · Based on the Novel by
RAFAEL SABATINI · Directed by **GEORGE SIDNEY** · Produced by **CAREY WILSON** · An M-G-M PICTURE

Janet Leigh, Stewart Granger (1952 portrait lobby card)

IVANHOE

(METRO-GOLDWYN-MAYER — 1952)

CAST: Robert Taylor, Elizabeth Taylor, Joan Fontaine,
George Sanders, Emlyn Williams, Robert Douglas, Finley Currie,
Felix Aylmer, Guy Rolfe
PRODUCER: Pandro S. Berman
DIRECTOR: Richard Thorpe
SCREENPLAY: Noel Langley; adapted by Aeneas MacKenzie from the
novel by Sir Walter Scott
DIRECTOR OF PHOTOGRAPHY: Frederick A. Young
106 minutes / Technicolor

One-sheet (1952)

The first, best, and most successful of Robert Taylor's MGM trilogy of European-filmed knights-in-armor spectacles (all produced by Pandro S. Berman and directed by Richard Thorpe) is *Ivanhoe*. This eye-filling and reasonably faithful screen adaptation of Sir Walter Scott's (1771–1832) 1819 historical novel is set in Norman-dominated England during the period of King Richard the Lion-hearted's captivity in Austria (1192–1194). Taylor, as disgraced Saxon knight, Wilfred of Ivanhoe, blends in reasonably well with the otherwise British-accented cast of beauties (Elizabeth Taylor and Joan Fontaine) and baddies (George Sanders, Robert Douglas, and Guy Rolfe).

Ivanhoe was the biggest production ever attempted in England up to that time. Full opposing armies had to be cast, outfitted, and trained in the use of medieval weaponry. A full-scale castle replica (Torquilstone Castle) with a ten-foot-deep moat was constructed on acreage at Boreham Wood Studios for the elaborate siege finale.

Its Cinemascope successor, *Knights of the Round Table* (art on pages 72–73), is an action-filled, but empty, retelling of the Camelot story with Taylor as Lancelot, Ava Gardner as Guinevere, and Mel Ferrer as King Arthur. Its one truly magnificent moment: an exhilarating single-take tracking shot with a horde of knights as they accelerate en masse from trot to gallop to full charge across a flat English plain. The studio took even further liberties with Taylor's ancestry by casting him as an American-accented Scottish mercenary in fifteenth century France in its version of Scott's 1823 romance, *The Adventures of Quentin Durward* (art on page 73).

The colorful collection of movie poster art presented on these three similar films compares the one-sheets and title cards from each. The Australian one-sheet on page 72 is a handsomely executed stone lithograph. The photo montage title cards from *Knights of the Round Table* and *Quentin Durward* are typical of MGM's mid-1950's style for these items and similarly-configured half-sheets.

Title card (1952)

One-sheet (1962 reissue)

One-sheet (1954—Australian)

Title card (1954)

Title card (1955)

One-sheet (1955)

THE ROBE

(TWENTIETH CENTURY-FOX — 1953)

CAST: Richard Burton, Jean Simmons, Victor Mature,
Michael Rennie, Jay Robinson, Dean Jagger, Torin Thatcher,
Richard Boone, Jeff Morrow, Dawn Addams
PRODUCER: Frank Ross
DIRECTOR: Henry Koster
SCREENPLAY: Philip Dunne; based on the novel by Lloyd C. Douglas
MUSIC: Alfred Newman
DIRECTOR OF PHOTOGRAPHY: Leon Shamroy
135 minutes / Technicolor / Cinemascope

One-sheet (1953—restored on linen)

Fox studio head Darryl F. Zanuck shrewdly hedged the company's bet on new widescreen process Cinemascope with his choice of the first project to be produced utilizing it. (For an explanation of Cinemascope consult the by-the-numbers explanation on page 75 opposite.) He knew that the late clergyman Lloyd C. Douglas (1877–1951) was the most widely-read author of *all time* by virtue of a series of "inspirational" bestsellers. The most colossally-consumed was, of course, *The Robe*, which was still on the best-seller lists *ten years* after its 1942 publication. The Zanuck formula of pre-sold-Douglas plus newfangled-Cinemascope equaled a staggering $20 million in U.S film rentals, a soaring send-off for this widescreen process, and booming audience demand for big screen, event-style spectacles.

Pack an extra toga, though, because this is the heaviest-spiritual-sledding of all the major Biblical pageants. It's *Quo Vadis* all over again with yet another leering Roman officer, Marcellus Gallio (Richard Burton), meeting a nice Christian girl, Diana (Jean Simmons), and deciding on the spur of the moment to get martyred. The catalyst for all this redemption is *The Robe* which belonged to Jesus Christ when he was crucified by a Roman detail led by Marcellus. Also present at Calvary is Marcellus' slave, Demetrius (Victor Mature), who flees with what soon becomes a much sought-after garment by Emperor Caligula (Jay Robinson) himself. Despite the important look of the gleaming marble production design, much of the film's credibility rests on simple close-ups of a divinely-drenched Mature wordlessly agonizing over Christ's final moments on earth. (See Jean Simmons' comments regarding *The Robe* on page 11.)

The sequel, *Demetrius and The Gladiators* (U.S. rentals: $4.5 million) (art on pages 74–75), features numerous gladiators agonizing over their own final moments on earth after they, and a helpful screenplay, temporarily turn Demetrius into an unstoppable arena killing machine. Sultry Susan Hayward joins this installment as Demetrius' leading fan, Messalina.

Pressbook detail (1953)

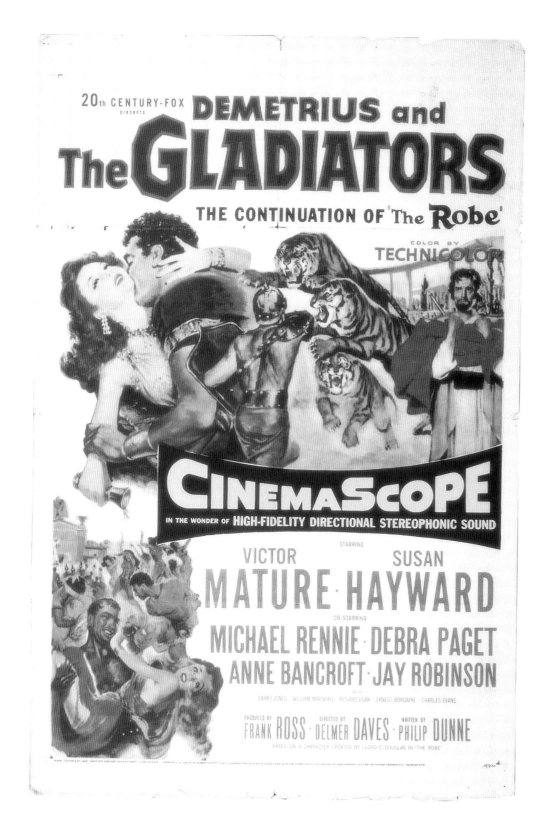

One-sheet (1954—unrestored)

Susan Hayward, Victor Mature, Ernest Borgnine

Jay Robinson, Victor Mature

Demetrius and the GLADIATORS

CINemaScopE
In The Wonder Of HIGH-FIDELITY DIRECTIONAL-STEREOPHONIC SOUND

starring

**VICTOR
MATURE**

**SUSAN
HAYWARD**

co-starring

MICHAEL RENNIE

DEBRA PAGET

ANNE BANCROFT

JAY ROBINSON

with

BARRY JONES · WILLIAM MARSHALL · RICHARD EGAN
ERNEST BORGNINE · CHARLES EVANS

Produced by

FRANK ROSS

Directed by

DELMER DAVES

Written by

PHILIP DUNNE

20th CENTURY FOX

BASED ON A CHARACTER CREATED
BY LLOYD C. DOUGLAS IN "THE ROBE"

COLOR BY **TECHNICOLOR**

Victor Mature (1954 lobby card)

LAND OF THE PHARAOHS

(WARNER BROS. — 1955)

CAST: Jack Hawkins, Joan Collins, Alexis Minotis, Sydney Chaplin,
James Robertson Justice, Dewey Martin, Luisa Boni, James Hayter
PRODUCER/DIRECTOR: Howard Hawks
SCREENPLAY: William Faulkner, Harry Kurnitz, and Harold Jack Bloom
MUSIC: Dimitri Tiomkin
DIRECTORS OF PHOTOGRAPHY: Lee Garmes and Russell Harlan
104 minutes / WarnerColor / Cinemascope

One-sheet (1955)

Land of the Pharaohs is a supremely glitzy slab of ancient Egyptian pomp that goes so far overboard in spectacularly re-enacting the construction of the Great Pyramid at Giza that the film approaches semi-documentary status.

Producer-director Howard Hawks, second unit director Noel Howard, and a double load of A-list directors of photography traveled to Egypt to stage the sprawling spectacle of an entire people at work on a monument to a man who believed he *could* take it with him. The Warner Bros. pressbook claims that one sequence filmed by Hawks at the famous ancient granite quarries at Tourah, Egypt, featured 9,787 extras: 5,260 Egyptian extras, 3,270 soldiers, and 257 atmosphere and bit players.

The film's fiercest display of spectacle, however, is its first, the Pharaoh's (Jack Hawkins) triumphant return procession through the city with his army. Hawks' camera dollies along with Hawkins as he's borne in a sedan carried by eight bearers, which itself is borne on a giant sedan carried by a further forty bearers. Composer Dimitri Tiomkin mockingly hurls every piece of brass in the orchestra pit at this vaultingly conspicuous display of might, but one still gapes with envy: it's good to be Pharaoh. The lavish palace interiors were filmed at Cinecitta Studios in Rome.

The trashy and compact storyline (which credits novelist William Faulkner as one of the writers) moves forward in brusque strokes. It's lash at first sight when the fetching Nellifer, Princess of Cypress (Joan Collins in full headstrong sex siren mode) cops a flogging from Pharaoh for her petulance while trying to trade her body to him in place of the tribute her people owe. In no time, greedy Nelifer becomes his queen and begins coveting the treasure her husband plans to seal in the crypt with his remains. The finale inside the self-closing pyramid is a pip.

The one-sheet on this page represents the later days of the Warner Bros. photography based posters. (Value: $35.) The lobby card on page 79 suggests the iridescent costumes.

Joan Collins, James Hayter (1955 lobby card)

HELEN OF TROY

(WARNER BROS. — 1956)

CAST: Rosanna Podesta, Jacques Sernas, Sir Cedric Hardwicke, Stanley Baker, Niall MacGinnis, Robert Douglas, Nora Swinburne, Torin Thatcher, Harry Andrews, Ronald Lewis, Janette Scott, Brigitte Bardot, Robert Brown, Maxwell Reed, Marc Lawrence
DIRECTOR: Robert Wise
SCREENPLAY: John Twist and Hugh Gray
MUSIC: Max Steiner
DIRECTOR OF PHOTOGRAPHY: Harry Stradling
116 minutes / WarnerColor / Cinemascope

One-sheet (1956—unrestored)

One of the signature aspects of producer-director Robert Wise's body of work is its impressive range. Ponder the stretch from *The Day the Earth Stood Still* (1951) to *The Sound of Music* (1965). Wanting to try his hand at the challenges of Cinemascope, Wise accepted Warner Brothers' offer to direct (and de facto produce) a historical epic based on Homer's ninth century B.C. epic poem, *The Iliad*, to be mounted at Cinecitta Studios in Rome.

From a sheer production perspective, *Helen of Troy* is a superior spectacle. For starters, it's one of the few ancient epics production designed around Greek culture instead of Roman. Wise and company researched a Minoan design for the vaulting walls and city of Troy and a Doric one for scenes set at court in Sparta. The authentic blacks, olives, and terra cottas predominating the decor and costumes give the film an uncluttered, classical look and feel. Given his deep cast of some of the most stalwart British players of the day, Wise opted to carefully dub British-accented voices for Continental-born leads Rosanna Podesta (Italian) and Jacques Sernas (Lithuanian). The ploy succeeds handsomely, but the film still plays more as an ensemble piece than the sweeping love story of Trojan Paris and the impossibly beautiful Helen of Sparta, whose adultery triggers the ten-year Trojan War. Especially memorable are Stanley Baker's atavistic Achilles and Niall MacGinnis' smoldering turn as cuckold King Menelaus.

Wise delegated responsibility for the film's major set piece—the Greeks' full frontal assault on the impregnable walls of Troy—to the fortuitously-combined skills of legendary second unit director Yakima Canutt and leading action director Raoul Walsh (who happened to be in Europe and owed Warner Bros. workdays under his studio contract). Their seven-minute wing-ding of a siege of Troy is every epic movie poster brought to life, every outrageous copy proclamation fulfilled. Well-trained and equipped stuntmen and extras in superb armor hack away at each other in a spectacular attack and fiery retreat ranking with the best in the cycle.

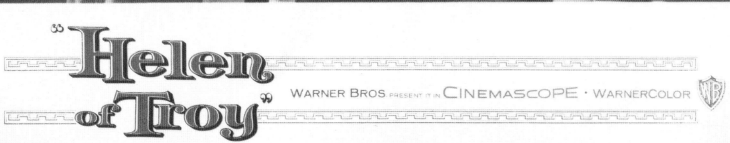

WARNER BROS PRESENT IT IN CINEMASCOPE · WARNERCOLOR

1

56 \ 52

Sir Cedric Hardwicke, Nora Swinburne, Janette Scott, Jacques Sernas, Rosanna Podesta (1956 lobby card)

THE TEN COMMANDMENTS

(PARAMOUNT — 1956)

CAST: Charlton Heston, Yul Brynner, Anne Baxter, Edward G. Robinson, Yvonne De Carlo, Debra Paget, John Derek, Sir Cedric Hardwicke, Nina Foch, Martha Scott, Judith Anderson, Vincent Price
PRODUCED BY MOTION PICTURE ASSOCIATES, INC.
PRODUCER/DIRECTOR: Cecil B. DeMille
SCREENPLAY: Aeneas MacKenzie, Jesse L. Lasky, Jr., Jack Garris, and Fredric M. Frank
MUSIC: Elmer Bernstein
DIRECTOR OF PHOTOGRAPHY: Loyal Griggs
221 minutes / Technicolor / VistaVision

One-sheet (1956—style A)

Still one of the most famous motion pictures of all time, producer-director Cecil B. DeMille's final epic, *The Ten Commandments*, is as grandiose a monument to DeMille's style as the pyramids are to the ancient Pharaohs. The incredibly demanding role of Moses also installed actor Charlton Heston as the enduring embodiment of epic film. DeMille's standard cinematic vices and virtues flourish in this all-star living Bible of a movie. (DeMille's titles for the 1923 silent version cited *chapter and verse*.) It also boasts one of the cinema's most revered set pieces, the Exodus from Egypt and (Academy Award-winning) parting of the Red Sea. As a last grandstanding hurrah, DeMille spent one million dollars staging the sequence in Egypt with over twelve thousand extras and fifteen hundred animals.

The contrasts between DeMille's 1923 silent version of *The Ten Commandments* and the deluxe 1956 edition are notable. Structurally, the last fifty minutes of the Heston version are actually *the first* fifty minutes of the silent, which uses the Exodus from Egypt segment as a lengthy prologue to a then-contemporary parable about obeying the commandments. An utterly gratuitous display of spectacle, this prologue is, nevertheless, DeMille's most masterful and exhilarating piece of period filmmaking. The silent's Moses (DeMille perennial Theodore Roberts) is presented as an aged patriarch who enters Egypt and confronts the sphinx-like, utterly heartless Rameses the Magnificent (obscure actor Charles De Roche in a stunning piece of screen villainy) demanding that he free the Hebrews. The 1956 blockbuster offers Moses' full life story. Here, the Hebrew foundling Moses (played by Heston's infant son, Fraser) is raised by the Egyptian royal family and later discovers his true heritage and destiny.

The style A one-sheet depicted on this page is not as sought after as style B, which features rich portraits of Heston as Moses and Yul Brynner as Rameses. Handsome, totally new poster art was created for each of the film's numerous reissues in the 1960s and 1970s.

Heston, Brynner, Hardwicke, Baxter

The Hebrews labor

The Hebrews flee

Charlton Heston

THE BRIDGE ON THE RIVER KWAI

(COLUMBIA — 1957)

CAST: William Holden, Alec Guinness, Jack Hawkins,
Sessue Hayakawa, James Donald, Geoffrey Horne, Andre Morell
PRODUCER: Sam Spiegel
DIRECTOR: David Lean
SCREENPLAY: Pierre Boulle (from his novel), Michael Wilson,
Carl Foreman
MUSIC: Malcolm Arnold
DIRECTOR OF PHOTOGRAPHY: Jack Hildyard
161 minutes / Technicolor / Cinemascope

Horne, Hawkins, Holden (1958 lobby card)

Location, location, location. *The Bridge on the River Kwai* immerses the viewer in a World War II Japanese prisoner of war labor camp deep in the sweltering Burmese jungle and then turns up the heat. The intricate blend of raw adventure and meticulously-orchestrated personal drama earned the film seven Academy Awards including Best Picture, Director, Actor (Alec Guinness), and Adapted Screenplay.

David Lean was an unemployed internationally-revered British director (*Great Expectations, Oliver Twist*) when his love of location filmmaking stranded him, much to his delight, in Ceylon (Sri Lanka) for almost a year creating *River Kwai*. This predilection for protracted shoots on remote, often difficult locations was Lean's true artistic secret weapon and the reason why this, and his succeeding super-epics (*Lawrence of Arabia, Doctor Zhivago, Ryan's Daughter, A Passage to India*) are imbued with unmatched authenticity. Counter-balancing Lean's propensity to go native was Galician-born independent producer Sam Spiegel. Spiegel had taken advantage of the decline of the studio contract system to position himself as the purveyor of such Academy Award-winning landmarks as *The African Queen* (1951) and *On the Waterfront* (1954).

Guinness portrays Colonel Nicholson, the commanding officer of a company of British prisoners-of-war forced to build a bridge over the River Kwai section of the Bangkok-Rangoon railway. When camp commander Colonel Saito (Sessue Hayakawa) orders all officers to perform labor in contravention of the Geneva Convention, he and Nicholson engage in a devastating battle of wills. William Holden co-stars as Sears, Nicholson's wry American co-captive, a character Spiegel suggested be added to the screenplay. Sears escapes, survives, but quickly has the smile wiped off his face when he is sent back to the jungle with zealous Major Warden (Jack Hawkins) and untested Lieutenant Joyce (Geoffrey Home) to destroy the now-nearly-completed bridge.

Despite the stellar international cast, the key art for the film, as depicted on the title card on page 85, is focused on the Bridge itself.

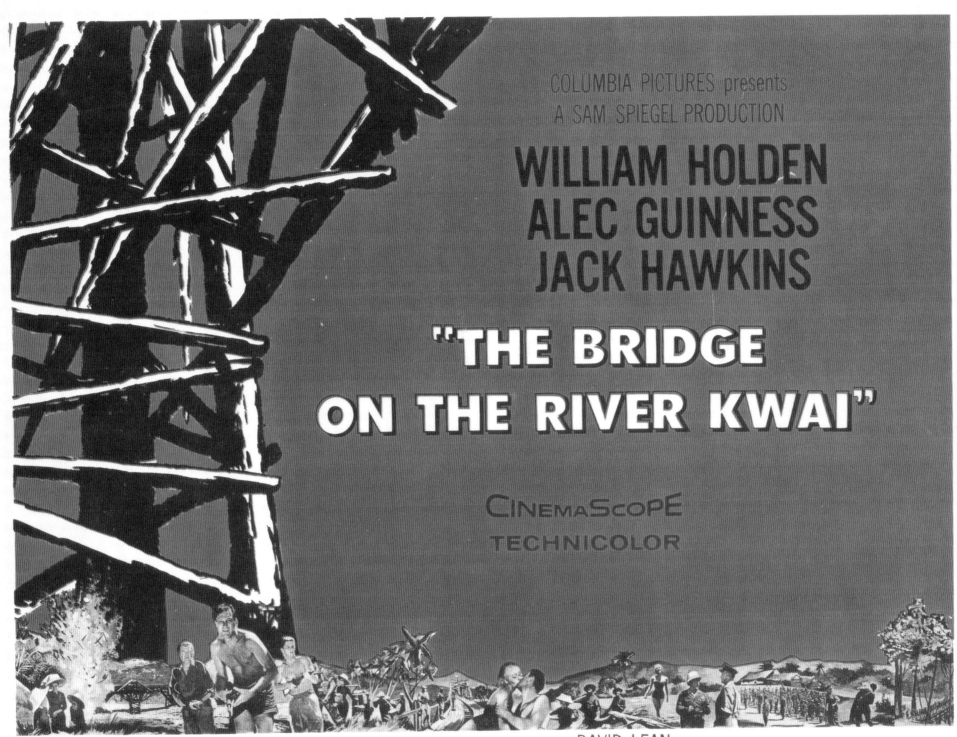

Title card (1958)

PATHS OF GLORY

(UNITED ARTISTS — 1957)

CAST: Kirk Douglas, Ralph Meeker, Adolph Menjou, George MacReady,
Wayne Morris, Richard Anderson, Timothy Carey, Joseph Turkel
A BRYNA PRODUCTION
PRODUCER: James B. Harris
DIRECTOR: Stanley Kubrick
SCREENPLAY: Stanley Kubrick, Calder Willingham, and Jim Thompson;
based on the novel by Humphrey Cobb
DIRECTOR OF PHOTOGRAPHY: George Krause
86 minutes / black and white

One-sheet (1958—restored on linen)

A full decade prior to the Vietnam era revisionism which would compromise the military's heretofore heroic movie image forever (see *The Sand Pebbles*, pages 110–111), Kirk Douglas' Bryna Productions (founded in 1955 and named after his mother) mounted this precisely-crafted, jewel box-sized anti-war epic. Humphrey Cobb's controversial true account of a shocking 1916 World War I court martial provided the raw material. A pair of twenty-nine-year-old independent filmmakers with a brilliant talent for black and white moviemaking named Stanley Kubrick and James B. Harris (who'd just completed 1956's *The Killing*) provided the visual style.

Douglas plays Colonel Dax, a decent-minded French officer with a civilian legal background, who is goaded by obscenely ambitious Generals Broulard (Adolph Menjou) and Mireau (George Macready) into leading a suicidal infantry attack against an impregnable German fortification nicknamed "The Anthill." Dax leads the first bloody wave into no man's land, but when the balance of troops refuse to advance, the offensive collapses. To avert disgrace, Mireau leads the next charge himself: to have three soldiers (Ralph Meeker, Timothy Carey, Joseph Turkel) selected as examples to be tried for the alleged cowardice of all. Mireau is ultimately exposed for having ordered French artillery to fire on his own hesitating troops, but the men are sacrificed nevertheless.

The black and white images of World War I's mud-caked trench life are recreated with a verisimilitude informed by the director's photojournalist's eye. The attack on "The Anthill" itself is a bravura piece of staging and fluid camerawork. Kubrick's gift for casting near-forgotten talents in major roles extends to Menjou and fading action hero Wayne Morris, who coughs up the performance of his career as alcoholic Lieutenant Roget.

Kubrick is briskly collected in movie paper circles. The silk screen-style one-sheet on this page currently auctions in the $600–800 range.

Title card (1958)

The attack on "The Anthill"

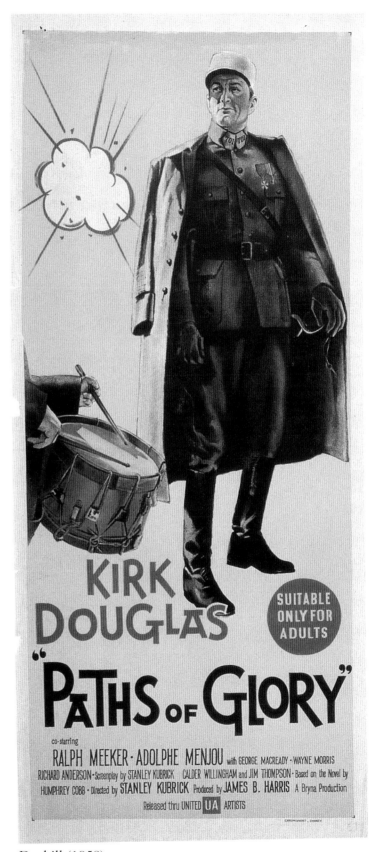

Daybill (1958)

THE VIKINGS

(UNITED ARTISTS — 1958)

CAST: Kirk Douglas, Tony Curtis, Ernest Borgnine, Janet Leigh, James Donald, Alexander Knox, Frank Thring, Maxine Audley
A BRYNA PRODUCTION
DIRECTOR: Richard Fleischer
PRODUCER: Jerry Bresler
SCREENPLAY: Calder Willingham; from the novel *The Viking* by Edison Marshall
MUSIC: Mario Nascimbene
DIRECTOR OF PHOTOGRAPHY: Jack Cardiff
114 minutes / Technicolor / Technirama

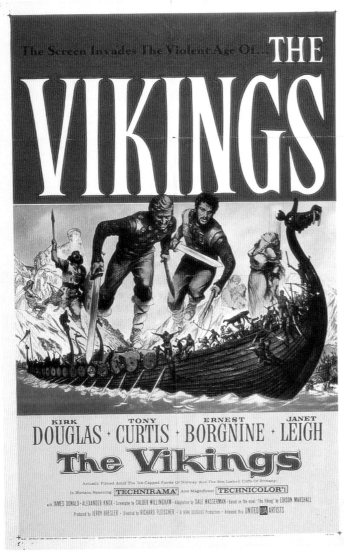

One-sheet (1958)

Movie-*Valhalla*-on-earth to its army of admirers, *The Vikings* is a boisterous and bloody tale of royal succession and revenge in ninth century England. Mercy is in short supply as the Norsemen of Long Sound, led by Ragnar (Ernest Borgnine) and his handsome, corrosive son, Einar (Kirk Douglas), target petty English despot Aella (Frank Thring) for plunder. They suffer a savage setback, however, when Aella captures Ragnar and pitches him to his personal pack of starving wolves. The enraged Einar stomachs a testy truce with his hated (secret) half-brother, Eric (Tony Curtis), and the vengeful Vikings cross the North Sea to lay siege to Aella's formidable bluffside castle and keep. Director Richard Fleischer's cobblestone by cobblestone taking of the fortress (Brittany's 700-year-old Fort LaLatte) is one of the highlights of the entire cycle. Don't miss it.

The real spectacle, in addition to the 30-acre Viking village constructed in Norway and the replicas of the Tube, Oseberg, and Gokstad Viking ships plying the fjords, is Kirk Douglas' swarming performance as Einar. Whether he's dancing from oar to oar on a long ship or crashing through a stained glass window on the end of a rope, this black-hearted warrior is one of Douglas' most robust screen creations. With this and 1960's *Spartacus*, Douglas, like Charlton Heston, transformed the super spectacle into a personal art form as well. Einar's almost perverse gentle side is passionately aroused by the captive Welsh Princess Morgana (Janet Leigh), who rejects him for Eric. "If I can't have your love, I'll take your hate," reasons Einar to Morgana as he prepares to hack Eric in two. (See *Trial by Combat* on page 31 for a description of *The Vikings*' climactic sword fight).

Movie poster material for *The Vikings* has never been readily available, although it is not costly when encountered. The one-sheet on this page sells for $100–200; the title card on page 89 sells for approximately $20–25.

Title card (1958)

BEN-HUR

CAST: Charlton Heston, Jack Hawkins, Haya Harareet, Stephen Boyd, Hugh Griffith, Martha Scott, Cathy O'Donnell, Sam Jaffe, Frank Thring
PRODUCER: Sam Zimbalist
DIRECTOR: William Wyler
SCREENPLAY: Karl Tunberg; based on the novel by General Lew Wallace
MUSIC: Miklos Rozsa
DIRECTOR OF PHOTOGRAPHY: Robert Surtees
217 minutes / Technicolor / Camera 65

Although he was referred to as General Lew Wallace (1827–1905), the ex-Civil War major-general who authored the 1880 novel *Ben-Hur: A Tale of the Christ*, was even more accomplished; he also served as governor of New Mexico (1878–1881) and minister to Turkey (1881–1885). A lengthy account of the spectacular travails of ancient Judean aristocrat Judah Ben-Hur, the novel was a phenomenal success in its day, eventually selling over two million copies. The stage version dramatized by William Young in 1899 (a scene from which is depicted on page 26) toured continuously until the early 1920s.

Metro-Goldwyn-Mayer produced an extraordinary silent version of *Ben-Hur* starring Ramon Novarro and Francis X. Bushman in 1925 (see art on page 29). This earnest, still-dazzling spectacle, which features several color sequences, follows the same storyline as the masterful 1959 super edition which earned an all-time high eleven Academy Awards for: Best Picture (Sam Zimbalist); Director (William Wyler); Actor (Charlton Heston); Supporting Actor (Hugh Griffith); Cinematography (color—Robert L. Surtees); Editing (Ralph E. Winters and John Dunning); Musical Score (drama or comedy—Miklos Rozsa); Art Direction (color); Costume Design (color); Special Effects (visual); Special Effects (audio).

The Wyler-Heston version, which was filmed principally at Cinecitta Studios in Rome, is a devout, splendidly-cast, richly exciting pageant of pageants. The climactic chariot race (executed after three months of planning by, once again, Yakima Canutt) remains the single most cathartic live action sequence ever shot.

The advertising campaign for *Ben-Hur* is almost as famous as the film, its massive stone letter motif duplicated by a number of subsequent epics (i.e. *El Cid*, see pages 98–99). It is presented here in a vertical style (one-sheet) and horizontal (title card). The original release one-sheet (without Academy Award references) sells for $150–200.

One-sheet (1960)

Title card (1960)

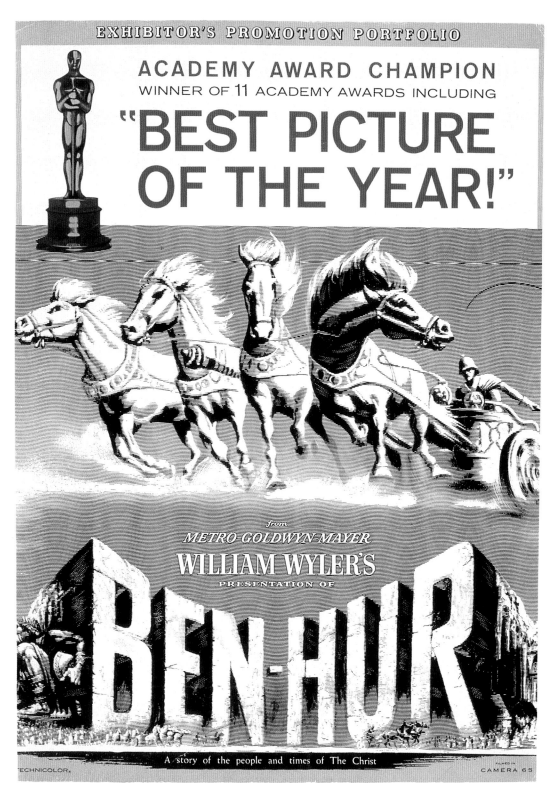

Pressbook cover (1960)

Stephen Boyd, Charlton Heston

Charlton Heston

The thrilling chariot race is about to begin. As all Rome cheers, Ben-Hur moves his team to the starting line.

from Metro-Goldwyn-Mayer
William Wyler's Presentation

TECHNICOLOR®
Camera 65

Charlton Heston (1960 lobby card)

SPARTACUS

(UNIVERSAL-INTERNATIONAL — 1960)

CAST: Kirk Douglas, Laurence Olivier, Jean Simmons, Charles Laughton, Peter Ustinov, John Gavin, Tony Curtis, Nina Foch, Herbert Lom, John Dall, John Ireland, Joanna Barnes, Charles McGraw, Woody Strode
A BRYNA PRODUCTION
EXECUTIVE PRODUCER: Kirk Douglas
PRODUCER: Edward Lewis
DIRECTOR: Stanley Kubrick
SCREENPLAY: Dalton Trumbo; based on the novel by Howard Fast
MUSIC: Alex North
DIRECTOR OF PHOTOGRAPHY: Russell Metty
RESTORED BY: Robert A. Harris and James C. Katz
196 minutes / Technicolor / Technirama 70

Spanish-language U.S. one-sheet (1960)

The universal theme of *Spartacus*, man's right to freedom, reverberates throughout the story of the film and the story in the film. In selecting blacklisted screenwriter Dalton Trumbo to adapt blacklisted novelist Howard Fast's 1958 account of the slave rebellion led by Thracian-born Roman gladiator Spartacus (?–71 B.C.), executive producer/star Kirk Douglas was making a courageous statement to the Hollywood establishment: end the industry's boycotting of creative talents whose careers were damaged or destroyed by the McCarthy-era investigations into alleged memberships in the Communist Party.

Trumbo delivered a witty, graphic, and moving screenplay from which the film's reputation as "the intelligent spectacular" partially derives. The narrative follows Spartacus from slavery in the Libyan salt mines, through to his brutal training at the Capua gladiatorial school, and on to his generalship of a doomed army of escaped slaves in what the Romans would dub the Third Servile War (73–71 B.C.). Douglas could have dominated the $12 million production with his force-of-nature performance (see *Trial by Combat*, page 31) but instead he hand-picked a regal cast of stars to uphold the credibility and scale of the conflict. (Read Jean Simmons' *Spartacus* recollections on page 11.)

Director Stanley Kubrick replaced director Anthony Mann after the commencement of principal photography, overseeing the balance of filming on the Universal back lot and in Spain, where the film's mesmerizing final battle was staged. Denied a Best Picture Academy Award nomination, *Spartacus* won four others: Best Supporting Actor (Peter Ustinov); Cinematography (color—Russell Metty); Art Direction (color); Costume Design (color).

Universal-International abandoned the Roman coin motif featured on the one-sheet on this page for the film's 1962 and 1968 reissues, but it remains the best art on the film.

Kirk Douglas, Woody Strode (Inside cover fold-out—soundtrack jacket—1960)

THE ALAMO

(UNITED ARTISTS — 1960)

CAST: John Wayne, Richard Widmark, Laurence Harvey, Richard Boone, Linda Cristal, Frankie Avalon, Patrick Wayne, Chill Wills, Joan O'Brien
PRODUCER/DIRECTOR: John Wayne
SCREENPLAY: James Edward Grant
MUSIC: Dimitri Tiomkin
DIRECTOR OF PHOTOGRAPHY: Bill Clothier
213 minutes / Technicolor

This rambling, sentimental, and, ultimately, stirring widescreen reenactment of the 1836 fortification, siege, and fall of the Alamo to the overwhelming forces of Mexican General Antonio Lopez de Santa Ana (1795–1876) is very much producer-director-star John Wayne's personal epic. The $7.5 million spectacle was nominated for seven Academy Awards (including Best Picture), winning one for Best Sound.

Wayne portrays frontier legend and politician Davy Crockett (1786–1836), who turns up with his rowdy backwoodsmen at the crumbling San Antonio, Texas mission being defended by volunteers led by Colonel William Travis (1792–1836) (Laurence Harvey) and namesake-knife-wielding Jim Bowie (1799–1836) (Richard Widmark). At that point, James Edward Grant's screenplay temporarily transforms itself into a broad Wayne-style western of the era (say 1961's *The Comancheros*, screenplay by, surprise, James Edward Grant). Generous gales of brawling and singing (by the likes of sorely-miscast teen idol Frankie Avalon) and a pointless romantic subplot involving Latin beauty Linda Cristal hobble the entire first one-third of the proceedings.

Tenacious viewers will remember *The Alamo*, however, especially its expertly-staged, thirteen-minute final assault on the $1.5 million mission replica Wayne had constructed in Bracketville, Texas. Reports of the star's longtime director and friend, John Ford (*Stagecoach*, *She Wore a Yellow Ribbon*), assisting in the mounting of this second-unit and special effects tour-de-force wouldn't appear to be untrue. The truly epic coordination of authentically-costumed Mexican troops, Alamo defenders, mass battlefield stunts, and blistering gun and cannon fire special effects render this segment a masterwork of its kind.

The linen-backed one-sheet on this page was illustrated by noted poster artist Reynolds Brown. While the one-sheet is readily available for $150–300, original lobby cards (and even reissue lobby cards like the portrait of John Wayne on page 97) are much more difficult to locate and are priced accordingly ($75–100).

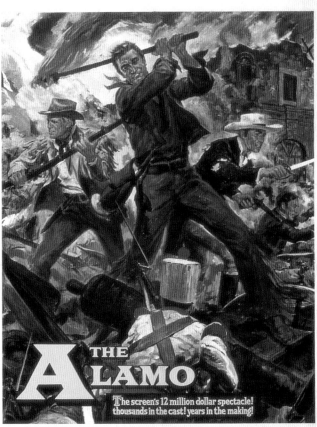

One-sheet (1960—on linen)

"THE ALAMO"

STARRING
JOHN WAYNE · RICHARD WIDMARK · LAURENCE HARVEY
CO-STARRING   AND GUEST STAR
FRANKIE AVALON   RICHARD BOONE   TECHNICOLOR®   A BATJAC PRODUCTION   RE-RELEASED THRU UNITED ARTISTS

John Wayne (1967 reissue lobby card)

EL CID

(ALLIED ARTISTS — 1961)

CAST: Charlton Heston, Sophia Loren, Raf Vallone, Genevieve Page, John Fraser, Gary Raymond, Hurt Hatfield, Massimo Serato, Herbert Lom, Douglas Wilmer, Frank Thring, Michael Hordern, Andrew Cruikshank
PRODUCER: Samuel Bronston
DIRECTOR: Anthony Mann
SCREENPLAY: Frederic M. Frank and Philip Yordan
MUSIC: Miklos Rozsa
DIRECTOR OF PHOTOGRAPHY: Robert Krasker
184 minutes / Technicolor / Super-Technirama 70

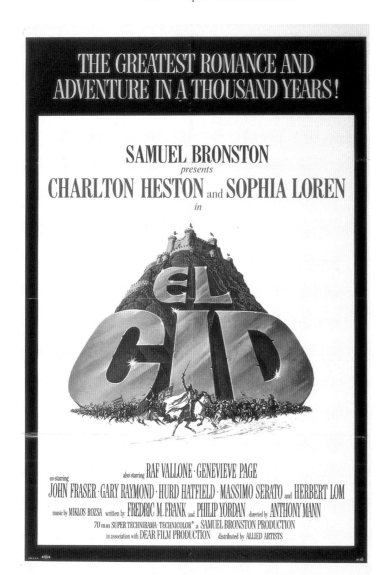

One-sheet (1961)

Between 1961 and 1964, Rumanian-born producer Samuel Bronston mounted five roadshow-style spectaculars on locations in Spain and at Samuel Bronston Studios in Madrid: *King of Kings* (1961); *El Cid* (1961); *55 Days at Peking* (1963); *The Fall of the Roman Empire* (1964); *Circus World* (1964). The best of show, *El Cid*, outclasses this field, and most others in the cycle, by dint of its sheer magnificence.

Charlton Heston portrays Spain's greatest hero, Rodrigo Diaz de Bivar (1030–1099), who was dubbed El Cid (the Lord) by the Moorish emirs he fought for and against. The film treats his exploits in asymmetrical chunks involving the turbulent early days of his marriage to the exquisite Chimene (Sophia Loren), his unsavory duties as Castilian champion to murderously-infighting royal siblings (Genevieve Page, John Fraser, Gary Raymond), and his capture and subsequent defense of the city of Valencia against the black-clad Moorish hordes of fanatical Ben Yussuf (Herbert Lom).

El Cid is one of the most fully-realized epics presented in this study. For most of his career its director, Anthony Mann, was a vastly-undervalued creator of definitive films noirs *(Raw Deal)* and stinging westerns *(The Man from Laramie)*. *El Cid* is his masterpiece. It should be savored for the charisma of its stars, the authenticity of such landmark Spanish settings as Belmonte and Peñiscola castles, and the verisimilitude of its displays of medieval personal combat and all out siege warfare.

Heston trained daily for two months with fencing master Enzo Musemuci Greco to accomplish the form he displays in the film's most gripping set piece: a thoroughly savage joust to the death to win the city of Calahorra. (See *Trial by Combat* on pages 30–31 for a further description of this quintessential genre encounter.)

As noted earlier, *El Cid* was branded with a *Ben-Hur*-style logo, though subsequent posters featured likenesses of Heston and Ms. Loren. The handsome one-sheet depicted on this page is readily available for $75–100.

Title card (1961)

Charlton Heston, Christopher Rhodes

Charlton Heston (German lobby card)

Hurd Hatfield, Charlton Heston

Sophia Loren, Charlton Heston

Charlton Heston, John Fraser

Charlton Heston, Sophia Loren (German lobby card)

THE LONGEST DAY

(TWENTIETH CENTURY-FOX — 1962)

CAST: John Wayne, Robert Mitchum, Henry Fonda,
Richard Burton, Robert Ryan, Peter Lawford, Curt Jurgens
(See complete list in pressbook detail below)
PRODUCER: Darryl F. Zanuck
DIRECTORS: Ken Annakin (British); Andrew Marton (U.S.);
Bernard Wicki (German)
SCREENPLAY: Cornelius Ryan; based on his book
MUSIC: Maurice Jarre
DIRECTORS OF PHOTOGRAPHY: Jean Bourgoin, Walter Wottitz
180 minutes / black and white / Cinemascope

Pressbook detail (1962)

Producer Darryl F. Zanuck's D-Day-sized recreation of the June 6, 1944 Allied invasion of Normandy is, somehow, the forgotten spectacular of the 1960s. A top international box office success in its day, Zanuck's greatest gamble might have been filming his $10 million 42-star production in black and white. The public was unfazed, as was Hollywood; this Best Picture nominee won an Academy Award for black and white cinematography. Also unlike its big-budgeted brethren, *The Longest Day* dared to offer subtitled scenes of its multi-national cast speaking in their native languages (i.e. the Germans speak German, the French French, etc.)

The power of *The Longest Day*'s complex and authentic amphibious and airborne assault reenactments is undiminished. Zanuck had two, and sometimes three, full production crews shooting at any of 31 locations up and down the Normandy coast. Among the action highlights is the scaling of Pointe du Hoc and a dazzling, extended single aerial take of the battle for Ouistreham.

The Longest Day also serves as a time capsule jammed with early-1960s male screen personalities. There are perennial American stalwarts John Wayne, Robert Mitchum, Robert Ryan, and Henry Fonda and a quartet of then-teen idols: Fabian, Paul Anka, Sal Mineo and Tommy Sands. Richard Burton, Peter Lawford, Kenneth More, Leo Genn, and Richard Todd round out the British contingent. Bristling with disbelief on the German side are the gleaming Curt Jurgens and Peter Van Eyck and Werner Hinz as Field Marshal Erwin Rommel. Other casting curios include a post-*Dr. No* Sean Connery, as a loquacious Allied invader and his *Goldfinger* co-star-to-be, Gert Frobe, as a German soldier.

The movie poster art for *The Longest Day* has its own daunting mission to accomplish: accommodating 42 alphabetically-ordered star likenesses. The 1970s German poster on page 103 offers illustrations of varying recognizability. From left to right we surmise them to be: Burton, Todd, Mitchum, Connery, Wayne, and Fonda.

German poster (1962)

German poster (1970s)

LAWRENCE OF ARABIA

(COLUMBIA — 1962)

CAST: Peter O'Toole, Alec Guinness, Anthony Quinn,
Jack Hawkins, Omar Sharif, Arthur Kennedy, Anthony Quayle,
Jose Ferrer, Claude Rains
PRODUCER: Sam Spiegel
DIRECTOR: David Lean
SCREENPLAY: Robert Bolt
MUSIC: Maurice Jarre
DIRECTOR OF PHOTOGRAPHY: Fred A. Young
221 minutes / Technicolor / Super Panavision 70

German poster (1962)

The winner of seven Academy Awards, including Best Picture and Best Director, *Lawrence of Arabia* remains one of the most vital, visual, masterfully crafted historical epics ever produced. Once again, director David Lean's delight in lengthy production schedules in remote, challenging locations served this eye-filling depiction of the fabled British officer's World War I desert exploits in spectacular stead.

Nearly two years of cinematography in desolate stretches of Saudi Arabia and Jordan (and on various sets constructed in Spain to double for 1916 Cairo, Damascus and Aqaba) resulted in rich, authentic backdrops for the sweeping proceedings. Finally, producer Sam Spiegel was compelled to all but *drag* Lean from the dunes after Columbia Pictures refused to advance further funds for the now-spiraling budget.

Based principally on Lawrence's 1935 memoir *The Seven Pillars of Wisdom*, the narrative concentrates almost exclusively on British Army Lieutenant T(homas) E(dward) Lawrence's (1885–1935) (Peter O'Toole) extraordinary rise from an obscure Arabian affairs post in Cairo to his stunning World War I successes as the desert strategist who unites the perennially mistrustful Arab bedouin tribal leaders (Alec Guiness, Anthony Quinn, Omar Sharif.)

Actor O'Toole was delighting audiences with his performance as Shylock in Peter Hall's Royal Shakespeare Company production of *The Merchant of Venice* when he was summoned by Spiegel to screen test in full Arab costume for the film career-making role of Lawrence. The pair had previously met in 1958 when O'Toole enraged Spiegel by cracking wise during a tense screen test for O'Toole to replace Montgomery Clift during principal photography of Spiegel's *Suddenly, Last Summer*. ("It's all right, Mrs. Spiegel, your son will never play the violin again." was the offending bon mot.) This time, O'Toole waited until the producer had formally offered him the role to ask: "Is it a speaking part?"

The *Lawrence of Arabia* movie art items juxtaposed here detail how posed, on-set production photographs (page 105) can serve as the basis for illustrated poster art.

Columbia Pictures presents THE SAM SPIEGEL · DAVID LEAN Production of

LAWRENCE OF ARABIA

A HORIZON PICTURE IN
TECHNICOLOR®

PHOTOGRAPHED IN
SUPER PANAVISION 70®

Peter O'Toole (1962 lobby card)

CLEOPATRA

CAST: Elizabeth Taylor, Richard Burton, Rex Harrison, Roddy McDowall, George Cole, Pamela Brown, Hume Cronyn, Cesare Danova, Kenneth Haigh, Andrew Keir, Martin Landau, Robert Stephens, Jean Marsh
PRODUCER: Walter Wanger
DIRECTOR: Joseph L. Mankiewicz
SCREENPLAY: Joseph L. Mankiewicz, Ranald MacDougall, Sidney Buchman; based on *The Life and Times of Cleopatra* by C.M. Franzero
MUSIC: Alex North
DIRECTOR OF PHOTOGRAPHY: Leon Shamroy
246 minutes / Deluxe Color / Todd AO

Spanish language U.S. one-sheet (1963)

Up until the mainstreaming of tabloid journalism in the 1990s, the most sizzling and protracted entertainment media *happening* of the century just might have been the worldwide attention focused on production of the 1963 spectacular, *Cleopatra*. The off-screen romance raging in Rome between stars Elizabeth Taylor and Richard Burton—while the film's unprecedented $40 million price tag was rocking Twentieth Century-Fox to its financial core—seemed to mirror the royal profligacy Hollywood costume epics normally recreated *on screen*.

Time has finally divorced the film from its feverish initial notoriety. What stands is a tasteful and enjoyably languid super spectacle best savored as a personality showcase for three major stars in their primes. Despite its marketing as a mega-glamor event featuring the then-most beautiful woman in the world, *Cleopatra* would also have to rank as one of Elizabeth Taylor's most challenging roles. The storyline is similar to earlier treatments of this historical triangle, with Cleopatra enchanting, in turn, Julius Caesar (Rex Harrison) and Mark Antony (Richard Burton) and facing the tragic aftermath.

Director and co-screenwriter Joseph L. Mankiewicz deserves tremendous credit for even undertaking, much less safely landing, this Boeing 747 of a movie. The structure alternates lengthy dialogue scenes in Alexandria and Rome with shimmering set pieces (the harbor at Alexandria, Cleopatra's entrance to Rome, Cleopatra's barge). Ms. Taylor gets ample screen time with both co-stars. Harrison, who got a mid-fifties career makeover after his success on stage in *My Fair Lady*, cruises through his role as Caesar. Burton has the far more bombastic one as Antony. Over time, *Cleopatra* recouped its massive budget and earned a profit.

The title card depicted on page 107 is part of a nine card roadshow lobby card set. It was reproduced in less lavish blue bordered and pink bordered sets for the film's general release in 1964.

Title card (1963)

THE GREAT ESCAPE

(UNITED ARTISTS — 1963)

CAST: Steve McQueen, James Garner, Richard Attenborough, Charles Bronson, James Coburn, Donald Pleasance, David McCallum, James Donald, Gordon Jackson
A MIRISCH-ALPHA PICTURE
PRODUCER/DIRECTOR: John Sturges
SCREENPLAY: James Clavell, W.R. Burnett; based on the book by Paul Brickhill
MUSIC: Elmer Bernstein
DIRECTOR OF PHOTOGRAPHY:
170 minutes / Deluxe Color / Panavision

One-sheet (1963—unrestored)

There were few 1960s moviegoing pleasures more complete than sitting back in one's seat and watching—and listening—to one of producer-director John Sturges' and composer Elmer Bernstein's pulsating action movie collaborations for films like the Mirisch Company's *The Magnificent Seven* (1960) or the Mirisch's subsequent prisoner-of-war camp blockbuster, *The Great Escape*.

The film is based on Paul Brickhill's 1950 account of his participation in the largest and most ingeniously-coordinated mass escape attempted by Allied prisoners of war during World War II. Steve McQueen, James Garner, Richard Attenborough, Charles Bronson, Donald Pleasance and James Coburn head a brimming cast of escape-aholic Allied prisoners-of-war whom the Germans have sequestered in a high security camp inside the Fatherland itself for what they hope will be the duration of the war. The full range of barbed-wire cliches and task-delineated stock characters are enhanced by a structure which spins-off and intercuts the characters' respective modes of escape as separate story strands once they're loose behind enemy lines.

Sturges had primed Steve McQueen's movie career by lifting him out of 1950s series television *(Wanted: Dead or Alive)* for his seminally cool gunfighting role in *The Magnificent Seven*. When he handed a motorcycle to McQueen for his exhilarating off-road race for freedom as Hilts in *The Great Escape*, he captured the mechanized lightning in a bottle which McQueen would transduce into international stardom. These long, fluid takes of McQueen gunning his stolen machine through impossibly scenic Alpine meadows with half the German motor pool up his rear reflector constitute movie mythmaking at its breathless best.

Unfortunately, none of the original movie poster or lobby card art from *The Great Escape* features McQueen on his motorcycle. The one-sheet on this page is one of the most desired pieces of movie paper on McQueen. (Value: $150–300 and rising.)

Steve McQueen (1963 lobby card)

THE SAND PEBBLES

(TWENTIETH CENTURY-FOX — 1966)

CAST: Steve McQueen, Richard Attenborough, Richard Crenna, Candice Bergen, Marayat Andriane, Mako, Larry Gates, Charles Robinson, Simon Oakland, Joseph Turkel, Ford Rainey, Gavin MacLeod, Gus Trikonis
AN ARGYLE-SOLAR PRODUCTIONS PICTURE
PRODUCER/DIRECTOR: Robert Wise
SCREENPLAY: Robert Anderson; from the novel by Richard McKenna
MUSIC: Jerry Goldsmith
DIRECTOR OF PHOTOGRAPHY: Joe MacDonald
182 minutes / Deluxe Color / Panavision

One-sheet (1966)

The winds of metaphor continually buffet producer-director Robert Wise's *The Sand Pebbles*, a majestic and heartbreaking cautionary tale set during the era of United States gunboat diplomacy on the Yangtze River in China, 1926. From the opening note of Jerry Goldsmith's main title theme, a pall of melancholy invests this story of the gunboat U.S.S. *San Pablo*, nicknamed the *Sand Pebbles*, and its increasingly fuzzy military objectives in a giant land hostile to even its puny presence.

Steve McQueen offers the simple and muted performance of his career as machinist Jake Holman, an uncomplicated loner who loves steam engines more than people. His uneasy period of transition to his new assignment on the *San Pablo* keeps him at odds with most of the tightly-knit crew of ugly American "China Sailors" (rich ensemble playing by Simon Oakland, Joseph Turkel, Ford Rainey, Gavin MacLeod and Gus Trikonis) for the duration of the drama.

The story concerns Holman and the young missionary who fancies him (Candice Bergen), his sailor buddy desperately in love with a Chinese woman (Richard Attenborough, Marayat Andriane), and the deteriorating fortunes of the *San Pablo* itself as it bobs with every swell in the choppy geo-political currents. The Vietnam metaphor of a stagnating superpower unable to wield its might decisively is tellingly put across. Richard Crenna appears as Lieutenant Collins, the gunboat's stentorian commanding officer. His dawning appreciation of what it now means to be a mere symbol of military power—rather than an instrument of it—leads him to order one last vainglorious mission up the Yangtze. Crenna's bracing, bristling performance has been overlooked for decades.

The Sand Pebbles was nominated for eight Academy Awards: Best Picture (Wise); Actor (McQueen); Supporting Actor (Mako); Cinematography (color); Art Direction (Color); Original Score (Goldsmith): Editing; Sound.

THIS IS THE HEROIC STORY OF
THE MEN ON THE U.S.S. SAN PABLO
WHO DISTURBED THE SLEEPING
DRAGON OF CHINA
AS THE WORLD WATCHED
IN BREATHLESS TERROR.

20th CENTURY-FOX presents

THE SAND PEBBLES

A ROBERT WISE PRODUCTION
STARRING
STEVE McQUEEN
RICHARD ATTENBOROUGH · RICHARD CRENNA · CANDICE BERGEN
ALSO STARRING
MARAYAT ANDRIANE · DIRECTED BY ROBERT WISE · SCREENPLAY BY ROBERT ANDERSON · BASED ON THE NOVEL BY RICHARD McKENNA · PRODUCTION DESIGNED BY BORIS LEVEN · MUSIC BY JERRY GOLDSMITH
ORIGINAL SOUND TRACK ALBUM
ON 20TH CENTURY-FOX RECORDS.
AN ARGYLE-SOLAR PRODUCTIONS PICTURE · FILMED IN PANAVISION® · COLOR BY DELUXE

Half-sheet (1966)

THE CHARGE OF THE LIGHT BRIGADE

(UNITED ARTISTS — 1968)

CAST: Trevor Howard, Vanessa Redgrave, John Gielgud,
Harry Andrews, Jill Bennett, David Hemmings, Corin Redgrave
PRODUCER: Neil Hartley
DIRECTOR: Tony Richardson
SCREENPLAY: Charles Wood
MUSIC: John Addison
DIRECTOR OF PHOTOGRAPHY: David Watkin
130 minutes / Deluxe color / Panavision

One-sheet (1968—heavy creasing)

Like *The Sand Pebbles*, the two decidedly non-Hollywood historical features discussed here reflect a late 1960s/early1970s shift in emphasis from pageantry to political commentary and satire in the period film.

On one hand, Tony Richardson's *The Charge of the Light Brigade* is a lush 1850s-set spectacle which pays homage to the types of set pieces found in its basically-unrelated 1936 namesake starring Errol Flynn and Olivia de Havilland. There are elegant balls at plush English country manors in which the stifling social rituals—and brazen randiness—of the military-worshipping upper classes (Vanessa Redgrave, David Hemmings, Jill Bennett) are sharply observed. This wafer thin gentility is contrasted with the unconscionable brutality of the discipline inflicted in the ranks of Lord Cardigan's (Trevor Howard) Light Cavalry Brigade as seasoning for the upcoming Crimean War (1845–1856). Yes, the 673 of the Light Brigade suicidally charge the Russian artillery at the Battle of Balaklava (1854) in this version too, but the point is made that with deluded blue bloods like Lord Raglan (John Gielgud) and Lord Lucan (Harry Andrews) running the trumped-up conflict, one shouldn't be surprised.

Burn! (original title: *Queimada*) is a carefully measured, 1830s-set companion piece to director Gillo Pontecorvo's gripping 1966 *cinema verite*-style political classic, *The Battle of Algiers*. Marlon Brando portrays William Walker, a British *agent provocateur* sent to the fictitious Lesser Antilles sugar colony of Queimada (Portuguese for *burnt*) to destabilize the situation so a group of local businessmen partial to Britain can seize power from the Portuguese. Walker discovers the spark of leadership in dock porter Jose Dolores (Evaristo Marquez), who becomes the successful "leader" of Walker's carefully-scripted insurrection. When Britain's economic priorities in the region change a decade later, Walker returns to Queimada to oust his protegee from power. Composer Ennio Morricone provides a wry musical score for this intriguing anti-epic. Savor it for yourself.

David Hemmings

Jill Bennett, John Gielgud

One-sheet (1970)

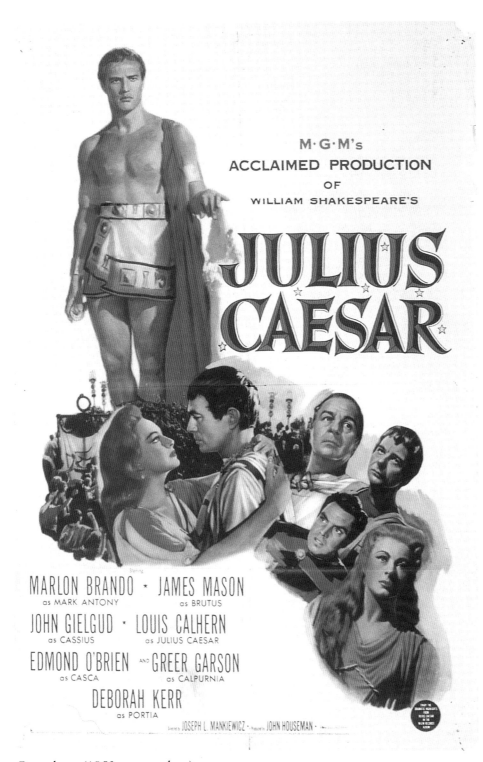

One-sheet (1953—paper loss)

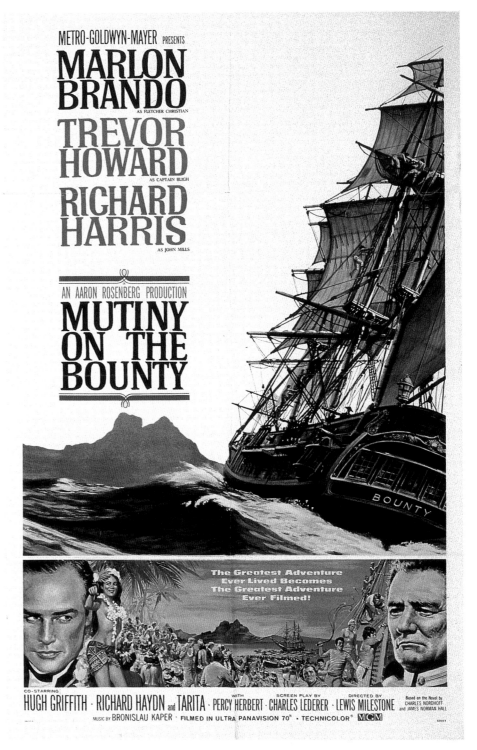

One-sheet (1962)

GALLERY OF FURTHER MAJOR EXAMPLES
(1932-1970)

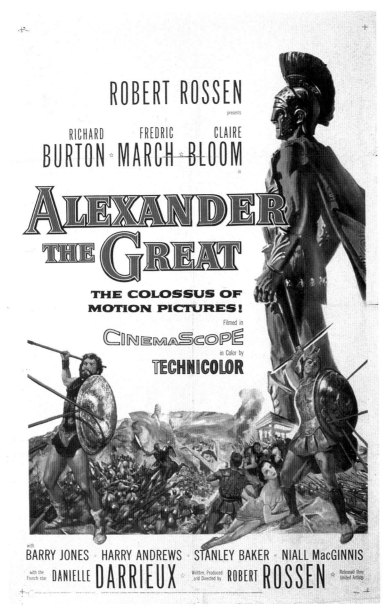

ALEXANDER THE GREAT
One-sheet (1956)

Richard Burton is the golden-tressed world-conqueror-in-waiting to Fredric March's deathly paranoid King Philip of Macedon in writer-producer-director Robert Rossen's episodic condensation of Alexander's exploits. Rugged locations in Spain double for ancient Macedonia, Greece, and Asia Minor.

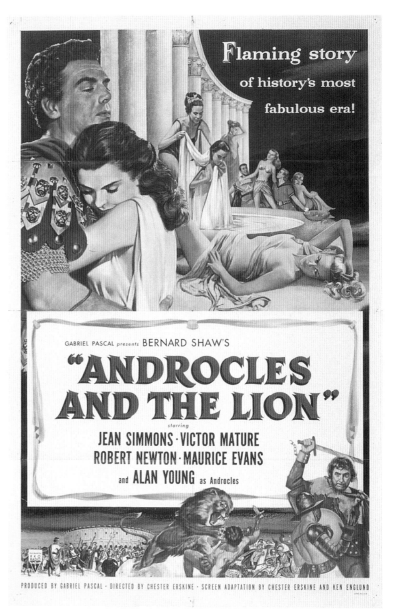

ANDROCLES AND THE LION
One-sheet (1953)

More satire than spectacle, RKO's screen version of George Bernard Shaw's play features Alan Young as a condemned Christian tailor whose past kindness to an injured lion in the wild benefits him when they re-meet in the arena during the era of persecution in ancient Rome. Jean Simmons is the devout beauty who melts the bronze heart of captain Victor Mature.

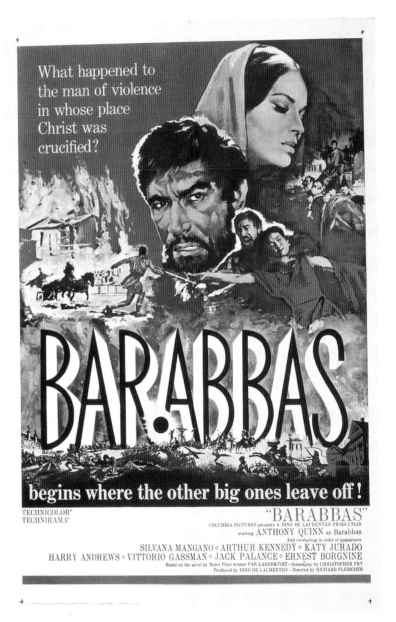

Around The World in 80 Days
One-sheet (1956)

Barabbas
One-sheet (1962)

Mike Todd's all-star production of Jules Verne's novel *Le tour du monde en quartre-vingts jours* was one of the premiere roadshow moviegoing attractions of the mid-1950s, capturing five 1956 Academy Awards, including Best Picture. Frank Sinatra, Marlene Dietrich, and Ronald Colman top the roster of famous cameo players encountered by cloud-hopping odd couple David Niven and Cantinflas.

Suddenly enmeshed in the Christ legend when he is spared crucifixion at Calvary by Pontius Pilate (Arthur Kennedy), the thief Barabbas (Anthony Quinn) toils in the Roman empire's lower depths (the sulphur mines and gladiatorial arenas) in search of spiritual redemption. Christopher Fry's adaptation of Par Lagerkvist's novel was filmed in Italy during the peak of the European costume movie boom.

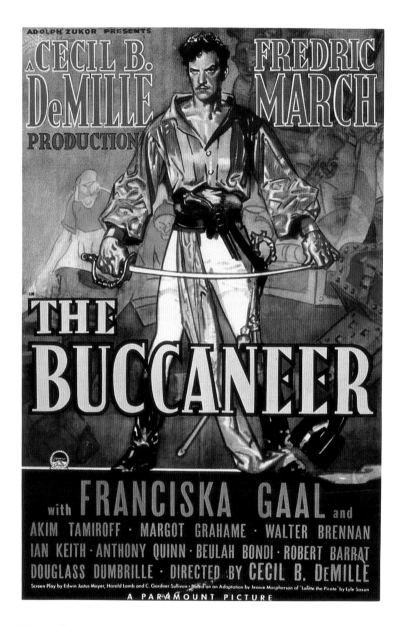

THE BUCCANEER
One-sheet (1938)

French pirate Jean Lafitte's powder and shot seals General Andrew Jackson's War of 1812 victory over the British at the Battle of New Orleans in Paramount's more medium-sized helping of American-history-a-la-DeMille.

THE BUCCANEER
One-sheet (1958)

Cecil B. DeMille's final production, a traditional backlot-mounted Technicolor remake of the 1938 original, was directed by his then-son-in-law, actor Anthony Quinn. While Charlton Heston had portrayed Andrew Jackson in *The President's Lady* (1953) for Twentieth Century-Fox, this supporting rendition of "Old Hickory" opposite Yul Brynner's Lafitte is among his signature historical characterizations.

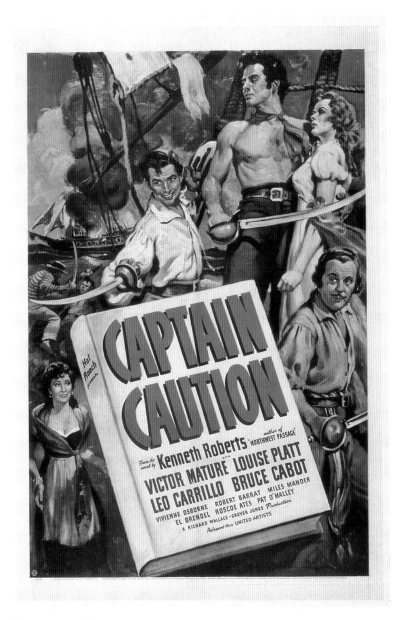

CAPTAIN CAUTION
One-sheet (1940—restored on linen)

The War of 1812 also provides the setting for this early Victor Mature seafaring opus for United Artists. Then-little-known actor Alan Ladd, two years away from his star-making role in *This Gun for Hire* at Paramount, can be glimpsed in a supporting role as one of the crew.

CAPTAIN KIDD
One-sheet (1945—on linen)

What might first appear from the richly-illustrated one-sheet to be a lusty pirate epic featuring Charles Laughton in some juicy period character turn is actually a disappointingly threadbare Grade B costume adventure of little reputation.

A CONNECTICUT YANKEE IN KING ARTHUR'S COURT
One-sheet (1949)

Like his frequent co-star, Bob Hope, Bing Crosby crossed over into the historical genre by means of musical comedy. A plush Technicolor pageant principally played for laughs, this third screen adaptation of Mark Twain's fantasy classic (the others: 1921 with Harry C. Myers; 1936 with Will Rogers) featured Jimmy Van Heusen and Johnny Burke songs for Crosby to croon with co-stars Rhonda Fleming and William Bendix.

THE CONQUEROR
One-sheet (1956—restored on linen)

Only a critic-proof titan like John Wayne could strap on a scimitar and a pointy tin helmet and still pillage the box office in his one and only *eastern*—as Genghis Khan, no less. His lust-hate wooing of Tartar beauty Bortai (Susan Hayward) suffers an embarrassing setback when she has him yoked to her wagon so she can whip him across the Gobi.

THE EGYPTIAN
One-sheet (1954)

The critics couldn't dissuade moviegoers from Twentieth Century-Fox's Cinemascope sand and soap opera about an earnest physician (Edmund Purdom) whose ministrations are used and abused by the Egyptian royal family. Its then-regal $6,000,000 in box office rentals made it the fourth highest-grossing film of 1954.

EXODUS
One-sheet (1960)

Producer-director Otto Preminger spent the 1960s mounting event-style adaptations of major novels, including Leon Uris's mega-bestseller of the day, *Exodus*. A panoramic, now-forgotten epic about the birth of the State of Israel, *Exodus* boasts vital performances by a picked cast and an Academy Award-winning score by Ernest Gold. Poster art by Saul Bass.

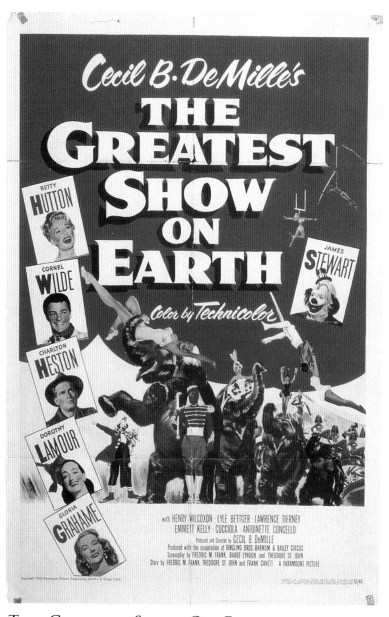

THE FLAME AND THE ARROW
One-sheet (1950)

Warner Bros.' vest pocket Robin Hood-style adventure set in the mountains of medieval Lombardy instantly established ex-acrobat Burt Lancaster as a swashbuckler with bounce. Working with former circus partner Nick Cravat, Lancaster nimbly neutralizes gravity in a series of delightful aerial set pieces in the castle of the despotic vassal who has abducted his son.

THE GREATEST SHOW ON EARTH
One-sheet (1952)

After decades of painstakingly duplicating exotic settings on backlots and sound stages, producer-director Cecil B. DeMille earned his only Best Picture Academy Award by renting somebody else's spectacle and filming that: the actual Ringling Brothers, Barnum, and Bailey Circus.

THE GUNS OF NAVARONE
One-sheet (1961)

Hollywood spent the next quarter-century unsuccessfully trying to mine gold out of Alastair MacLean high adventure novels the way screenwriter-producer Carl Foreman and director J. Lee Thompson did in this exemplary Blow-The-Big-Objective-Win-The-War-type blockbuster.

HOW THE WEST WAS WON
One-sheet (1963)

With composer Alfred Newman's main title anthem coursing through the soundtrack and three veteran directors wrapping the Cinerama screen around the faces of some of the biggest stars of the era, *How The West Was Won* chronicles three generations of one 19th-century American family's experiences Out West.

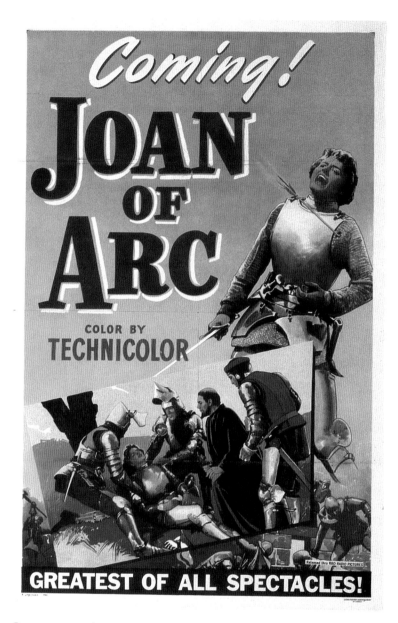

JOAN OF ARC
Teaser one-sheet (1948—style B)

Not even seven Academy Award nominations, including Best Actress
for star Ingrid Bergman, could sway the critical consensus that director
Victor Fleming's ornate screen adaptation of Maxwell Anderson's play
Joan of Lorraine distanced audiences with too much talk and too little
action.

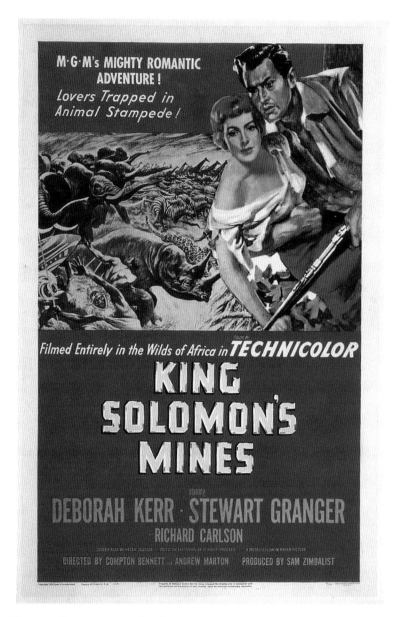

KING SOLOMON'S MINES
One-sheet (1950—restored on linen)

Stewart Granger shot to international stardom as gruff white hunter
Allen Quatermain in Metro-Goldwyn-Mayer's sturdy version of
H. Rider Haggard's 1885 novel about adventure fiction's most profitable
African safari. Robert Surtees's Academy Award-winning color location
footage was so rich that the studio incorporated it into three more jungle
programmers: *Watusi* (1959); *Drums of Africa* (1963); *Trader Horn* (1973).

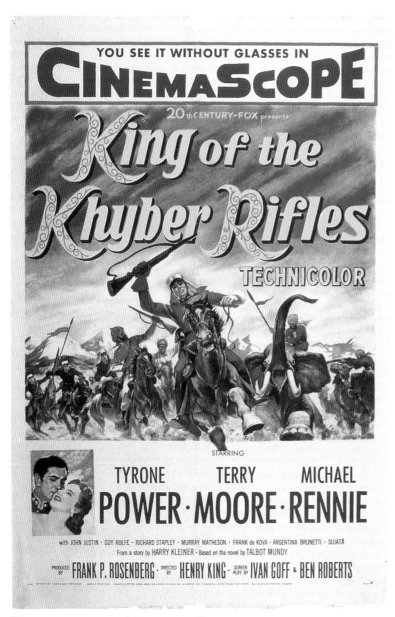

KING OF THE KHYBER RIFLES
One-sheet (1953—unrestored)

Twentieth Century-Fox dusted off the 1916 Talbot Mundy novel on which director John Ford had based its 1929 India epic, *The Black Watch*, and re-tooled it under its original title for Cinemascope and Technicolor as a latter day Tyrone Power-Henry King costume extravaganza.

KINGS OF THE SUN
One-sheet (1963)

The ancient Mayans get the full Mirisch Company action movie treatment, replete with an Elmer Bernstein score, in this ambitious, now-little-seen spectacle filmed entirely in Mexico. George Chakiris is the exiled chieftain who coerces captured North American native American Yul Brynner to help his settlers repulse invaders from their former homeland.

THE MAGNIFICENT SEVEN
One-sheet (1960)

Showcasing a clutch of the 1960s coolest anti-heroes-to-be—Steve McQueen, James Coburn, Charles Bronson, Robert Vaughn—the Mirisch Company's super-sized Mexican re-setting of Akira Kurosawa's *The Seven Samurai* is a benchmark for the large scale Hollywood western.

THE MAN IN THE IRON MASK
One-sheet (1939)

After a showy romantic role and early swordfight death in *Anthony Adverse* (1936), South African-born Louis Hayward settled into his metier in historical films in the dual role of frilly despot Louis XIV and the doubly-imprisoned owner-occupier of the iron mask.

PLYMOUTH ADVENTURE
One-sheet (1952)

Not surprisingly, Metro-Goldwyn-Mayer scheduled a Thanksgiving 1952 release date for their straightforward pre-Cinemascope depiction of the Pilgrims' historic crossing on the Mayflower.

THE PRINCESS AND THE PIRATE
One-sheet (1945)

Bob Hope interspersed his contemporary productions with period and genre spoofs as handsomely crafted as the films they lampooned (*Monsieur Beaucaire*, *Casanova's Big Night*). *The Princess and the Pirate* is typical of such Technicolor escapist fare with Hope and Virginia Mayo falling prey to some none-too-menacing pirates (Walter Slezak, Victor McLaglen).

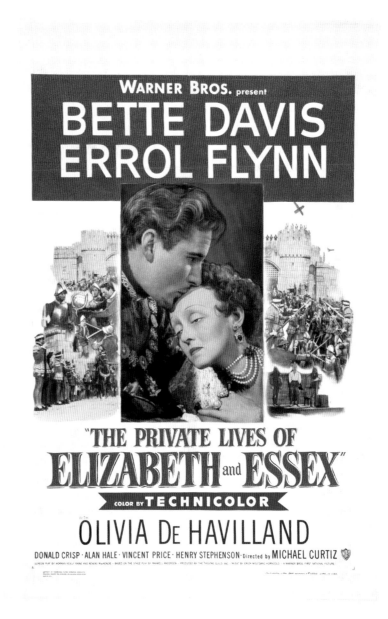

THE PRINCE WHO WAS A THIEF
One-sheet (1951)

Universal-International contract player Tony Curtis graduated to leading man status in this sleeper hit which revived the studio's production line output of Maria Montez-style backlot Baghdad costume adventures.

THE PRIVATE LIVES OF ELIZABETH AND ESSEX
One-sheet (1952 reissue—on linen)

An off-screen clash over billing and ego sabotaged whatever on-screen chemistry Bette Davis' Elizabeth I might have enjoyed with Errol Flynn's Lord Essex in Warner Brothers' nevertheless exquisite 3-strip Technicolor production. One of the great looking and sounding films from that magical Golden Age Hollywood year, 1939.

THE PRODIGAL
One-sheet (1955)

Metro-Goldwyn-Mayer loosed resident bad girl Lana Turner on
pagan times as gold digging high priestess Samarra in their Cinemascope
re-telling of the parable of the Prodigal Son. Edmund Purdom, who'd
tangled with idol-worshipping ancient beauties in *The Egyptian*, is
smitten until she quotes him her going spiritual rates.

SALOME
One-sheet (1953—restored on linen)

Where the Bible has sultry Salome perform the Dance of the Seven
Veils as a reward for receiving John the Baptist's head on a platter, this
third screen version (the others: Theda Bara, 1918; Alla Nazimova,
1923) sanitizes her legacy by positing that she danced to save him.
Either way, a mid-career Rita Hayworth pulls off the dance (and the
veils) with aplomb.

SEVEN SAMURAI
One-sheet (1982 reissue)

Akira Kurosawa's 1954 black-and-white feudal era epic about seven samurai warriors hired to defend a peasant village against marauding bandits is an example of—and a testament to—this unique body of Japanese historical cinema. The film received Academy Award nominations for Best Costume Design (black-and-white) and Best Art Direction/Set Decoration (black-and-white).

SIGN OF THE PAGAN
One-sheet (1955)

It's Attila the Hun (Jack Palance) versus Rome (Jeff Chandler) in a colorful backlot costume programmer which has some of the trappings—but none of the real spectacle—of the major screen epics of its day.

SOLOMON AND SHEBA
One-sheet (1959)

The production's original King Solomon, Tyrone Power, suffered a heart attack and died at age 45 on location in Spain while filming a swordfight with George Sanders. A brunette-wigged Yul Brynner was re-cast in the role, extensive re-shooting ensued, but Power still can be glimpsed in the final cut in long shots salvaged from his takes.

SUDAN
One-sheet (1945—on linen)

Ancient Egypt is resurrected in only the lower-budgeted aspects of its former glory in this last of the marvelously preposterous Technicolor costume fantasies featuring Maria Montez and Jon Hall. Their other Universal backlot mini-epics include: *Arabian Nights* (1942), *White Savage* (1943), *Ali Baba and the Forty Thieves, Cobra Woman, Gypsy Wildcat* (all 1944).

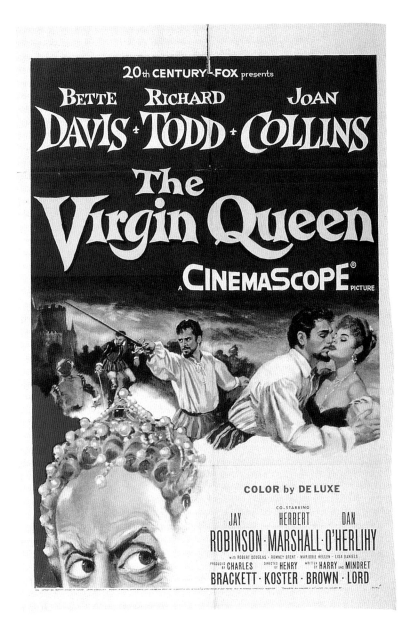

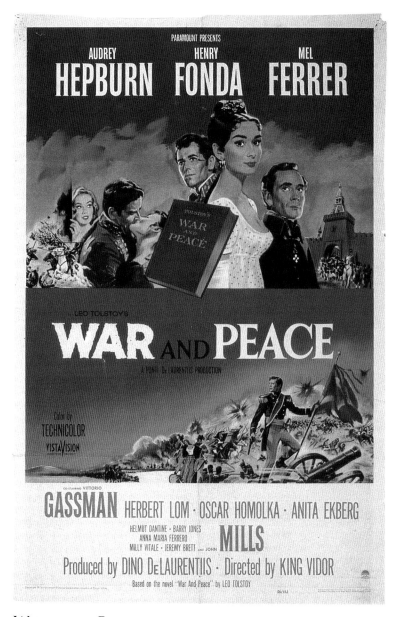

THE VIRGIN QUEEN
One-sheet (1956)

Not to be outdone by other screen Queen Elizabeths (Sara Bernhardt, Flora Robson—twice), Bette Davis solicited Twentieth Century-Fox's interest in having her reprise her *Elizabeth and Essex* role in their upcoming film on Sir Walter Raleigh. The studio consented and the project soon focused on you-know-who instead.

WAR AND PEACE
One-sheet (1956)

Huge formation battle sequences and Napoleon's disastrous winter retreat from Moscow are the real highlights of King Vidor's valiant attempt to condense Leo Tolstoy's leviathan of a novel into a meaningful moviewatching experience. A 373-minute Russian version directed by Sergei Bondarchuk won the Best Foreign Film Academy Award in 1968.

YOUNG BESS
One-sheet (1953)

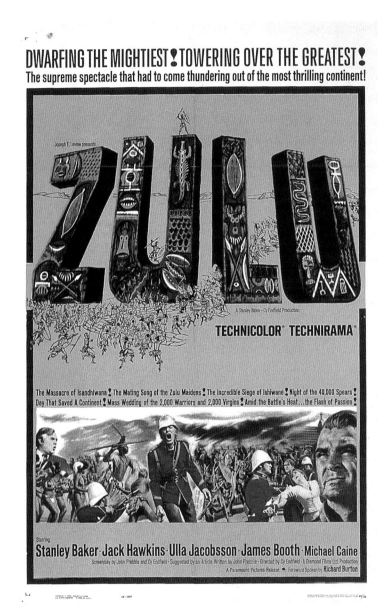

ZULU
One-sheet (1964)

Metro-Goldwyn-Mayer's toniest British cast of the decade played out the early days of Queen Elizabeth I (Jean Simmons) with Charles Laughton along for another screen ride as King Henry VIII. The autograph on the poster reads: *"This was one of my favorite films. Beautiful color costumes, story—and the stars . . . Stewart Granger"*.

Zulu is a gripping re-enactment of the miraculous 1879 Zulu War standoff between a small detachment of red-coated British infantry and the thousands of disciplined Zulu warriors they beat back in the famed Defense of Rorke's Drift, South Africa. One of the great battle films.

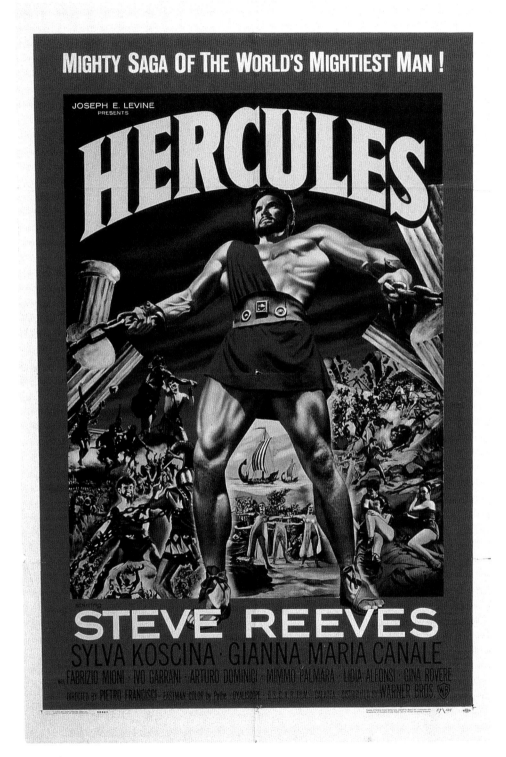

One-sheet (1959)

One-sheet (1960)

SWORD AND SANDAL SPECTACLES:
THE GREATEST ADVERTISING STORIES EVER TOLD

It began as a classic show business story of body and sell. The year was 1957. Italian film producer-director Pietro Francisci was seeking an actor with the face and physique to star as mythological strongman Hercules. Francisci had already sharpened his production skills on a number of earlier Italian "sword and sandal spectacles." "Sword and sandal spectacle" was an industry catchphrase for the steady stream of post-World War II, European-produced historical spectacles set during various ages of antiquity.

Sirens from across the centuries were often the protagonists of these frequently multinational co-productions. Examples include *Fabiola* (1951) with Michele Morgan, Francisci's own *The Queen of Sheba* (1953) with Eleanora Ruffo, and *Theodora, Slave Empress* (1954) with Gianna Maria Canale. With the exception of *Ulysses* (1955), which starred Hollywood import Kirk Douglas, none of these English-dubbed Euro-spectacles garnered much attention in the United States. Until *Hercules*.

HAVE BICEPS, WILL TRAVEL

Francisci's search ended abruptly one day when his 13-year-old daughter rushed home after seeing MGM's Jane Powell-Debbie Reynolds musical comedy *Athena*. "Daddy, I've found your Hercules!" she exclaimed. Francisci screened the film and then ordered a telegram and a plane ticket sent to one of the film's impressively-

Steve Reeves as Hercules (1959)

muscled, handsome supporting actors, imploring him to fly to Rome.

The wire was received in Los Angeles by a Montana-born (1926) former Mr. America (1947) and Mr. Universe (1950) named Steve Reeves. Reeves had just forsaken the mercurial fortunes of an acting career for a cushy, steady-paying promotion job with a national physical health chain, American Health Studios. A decade earlier, Cecil B. DeMille himself had signed the newly-crowned Reeves to a contract in hopes of grooming him to star in *Samson and Delilah*. Having subsequently completed supporting roles in features like *Athena* (1954) and cult director Ed Wood's *Jail Bait* (1954), Reeves now viewed Francisci's *Hercules* offer as the one chance he might ever have to star in a film.

Unlike earlier screen hulks, Reeves' sleek, high definition torso and leading man good looks would bring total freshness to the visual concept of gross physical strength. With his body the pivotal production value of the film, Reeves grew a beard, stripped down to a loincloth or peplum (a short, kilt-like male garment of ancient origin, hence the Italian nickname of these films—"peplum") and proceeded to master the martial arts of movie muscledom.

He contorted the Cretan Bull into cloven-hoofed carpaccio. He pulled down pagan temples with brutish panache. He flailed onrushing soldiers with a whirling length of broken chain, his signature stroke of movie mayhem. Upon completing his screen labors, Reeves flew back to the States and renewed his "day job."

If Reeves himself paid little attention to the end product, moviegoers across Europe did not share his indifference. *Hercules* quickly became the box-office rage of the continent.

JOSEPH E. LEVINE PRESENTS

The financial significance of this furor was not lost on one Joseph E. Levine. Levine was a New England film distributor who was concurrently masterminding the Stateside release of an earlier Francisci spectacle, *Attila* (1958), starring Anthony Quinn and Sophia Loren. Levine's company, Embassy Pictures, quickly ponied up $120,000 for the *Hercules* distribution rights. The late-blooming mogul then interested Warner Bros. in lavishing the kind of splashy multi-million dollar promotional budget on his low-priced Italian "pickup" that it reserved for its own major releases.

And what kind of movie were Levine and Warner Bros. about to front-end load into nearly a thousand theatres? Stripped of hoopla, *Hercules* is an adequately produced, medium-budgeted costume adventure not unlike the aforementioned sword and sandal spectacles of the 1950s. The plot centers on Hercules' and his beloved Iole's (Sylva Koscina) embroilment in a royal power struggle in the city of Jolco. In retrospect, Francisci's Hercules character is the best screen hero Reeves was given to play. Even within his narrow acting range, Francisci and cinematographer Mario Bava captured an unexpectedly brooding aspect to Reeves which sold *Hercules* to audiences as convincingly as his deeds of demolishing-do.

The limitation of the film, and of most subsequent European-produced films for this cycle and the "spaghetti westerns" which followed, is the quality of the dubbing into English. The unconvincing "American" voices often supplied for European supporting players would clash with the supposed antiquity of the settings. This imbued the films with that rollercoastering watchability quotient so common to exploitation fare: the action set pieces featured so prominently in the trailer and television spots are separated by long stretches of uninvolving dubbed dialogue mouthed by unfamiliar performers.

Hercules suffers this fate despite Francisci's skill at visual storytelling. Reeves is the whole show, even when he is little more than on display. His actual Gary Cooper-like voice was dubbed into a more classically-intoned voice in all languages, including English.

SATURATION NATION

In the end, the film's real secret weapon was its release pattern. *Hercules* was one of the earliest beneficiaries of the transition to today's basic feature film distribution strategy: saturation booking. Instead of the then-traditional cycle of premiering major films in exclusive engagements and slowly releasing them into neighborhood theatres, saturation booking inaugurated the release of "product" simultaneously in as many theatres as possible. Gross big, gross early.

Another key component of the *Hercules* launch was selling the sell to the theatre sector. To this end, Levine hosted the "*Hercules* Exhibitor Luncheon" for a thousand exhibitors at the Waldorf-Astoria Hotel in Manhattan. Attendees were deluged with *Hercules* paraphernalia, including elaborate pressbooks and presskits further hyping the herculean hype.

This wide theatre break was supported by major advertising and publicity campaigns, including significant reliance on the industry's new heavy artillery, 30 and 60-second television spots. *Hercules* was ripe for this type of exploitation. Churning music and sound effects, titanically exaggerated narration, and prime cuts of Reeves dishing beefy rough justice heralded *Hercules*' hard body hard sell onto North America's mostly black and white television screens during the summer of 1959.

The critics were unimpressed. In its July 23, 1959, review *The New York Times* groaned ". . . the picture bears out little of the breathless excitement of its advance building. It is a slow-paced and stilted affair studded with routine spectacles that have been since movies immemorial."

A Boom Is Born

An oblivious public stormed the box office to the tune of $4.7 million in rentals. A new action film star and a new action film craze were born. Reeves went on to star in another eleven European-mounted spectacles in the next six years, including three more produced by Levine: *Hercules Unchained* (1960), *Morgan the Pirate* (1961), and *The Thief of Baghdad* (1961).

A legion of copycat mythological muscleman adventures starring nearly twenty different Reeves bulk-alikes stoked a production boom in Italy and Spain. Former 1950s-era screen *Tarzan* Gordon Scott led the field of mostly English-speaking actors and actor/bodybuilders performing in this onslaught of films centered on the exploits of ancient strongmen repeatedly named

Lunch on Levine (1959)

Hercules, Samson, Goliath, Maciste, Ursus or the son thereof. An honor role of such sculpted heroes would certainly include: Mark Forest, Richard Harrison, Brad Harris, Reg Park, Alan Steel, Dan Vadis, Roger Browne, Kirk Morris, Joe Robinson, Michael Forest, Ed Fury, Rod Flash (Richard Lloyd), Rock Stevens (Peter Lupus) and others.

Playing opposite this buffed battalion of leading hunks was a sorority of diaphanously draped pan-European beauties equally adept at playing princesses, priestesses, virgins or vamps. Sylva Koscina, Rosanna Podesta, and Gianna Maria Canale were among the most frequently-cast co-stars. Joining them were: Anita Ekberg, Rosanna Schiaffino, Sylvia Lopez, Chelo Alonso, Edy Vessel, and Liana Orfei.

The European costume film upsurge soon expanded beyond the peplums. Idle Hollywood stars suddenly found themselves being summoned overseas to season a

smorgasbord of internationally co-produced historical biographies, lower case biblical spectacles, and twilight-of-the-cycle swashbucklers. They included: Stewart Granger (*Swordsman of Siena*—see poster on page 145), Cameron Mitchell (*Erik the Conqueror*—see poster on page 145), Rory Calhoun (*The Colossus of Rhodes*—see poster on page 144), Victor Mature, Orson Welles, Lex Barker, Cornel Wilde, Jack Palance and others.

From 1959 to 1965, all the major Hollywood studios found room on their release schedules for a muscle epic or two, their new alternative to the fading A and B Hollywood westerns. The Reeves posters on pages 138 through 141, as well as the series of American and international posters on the pages beyond, detail the consistent blend of epic mural-like illustration and hyperbolic ad copy which characterize the main body of poster art for these films.

A unique window into the origins of independent American International Pictures' *Samson* and *Goliath* posters on pages 142 and 143 is provided by the memoir of A.I.P. co-founder Samuel Z. Arkoff.

In his book, Arkoff recalls how he and co-founder James H. Nicholson traveled to Rome and acquired, re-dubbed into English, and, most significantly, *retitled* these co-productions with fantastic, exploitation-style titles. *Sign of Rome* starring Anita Ekberg became *Sign of the Gladiator* (1959) (see poster on page 144) despite the absence of gladiator scenes in the original film. *Goliath and the Barbarians* (1959) (see poster on page 138) originally had nothing to do with a hero named Goliath but was essentially re-written in the English dubbing to reframe the story, setting and characters.

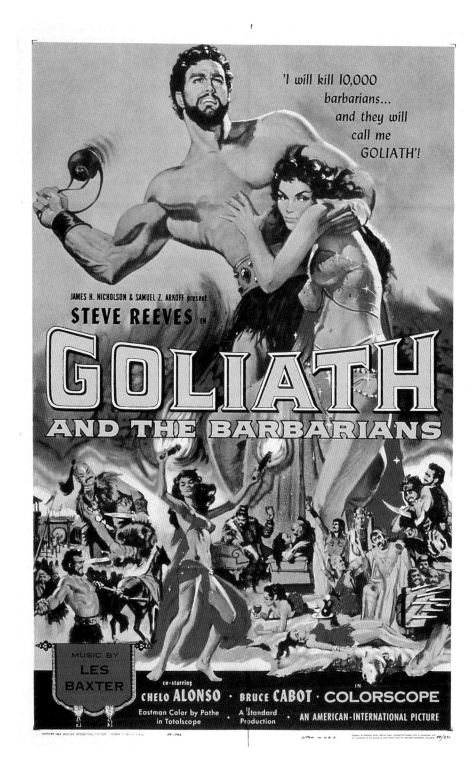

One-sheet (1959)

One-sheet (1960)

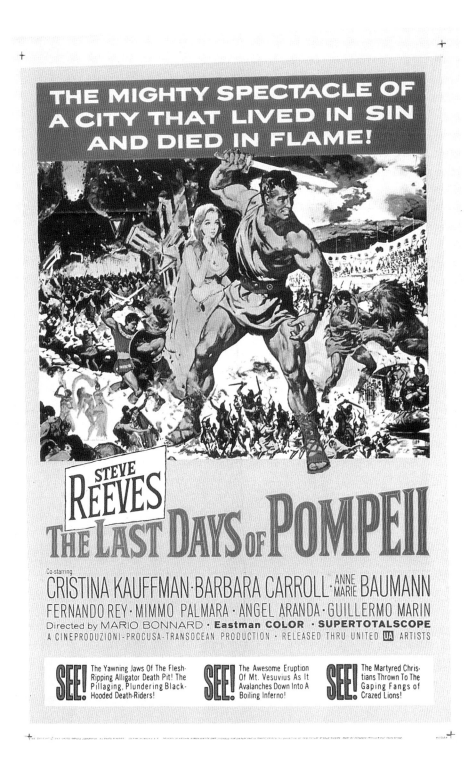

One-sheet (1960)

One-sheet (1961)

One-sheet (1961)

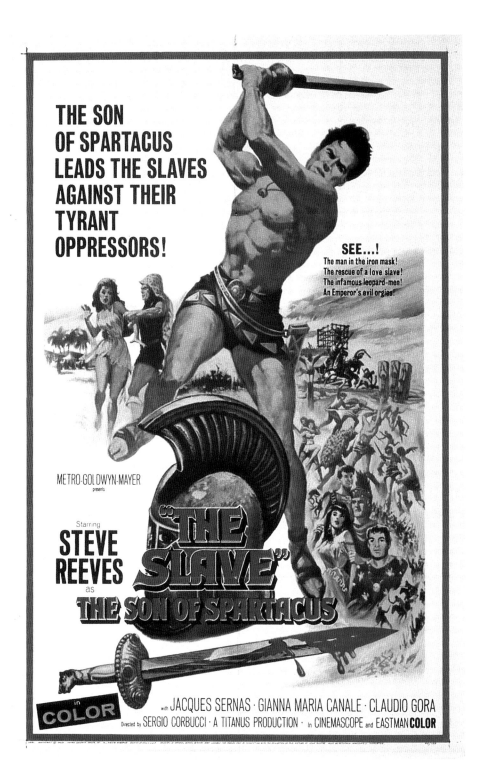

One-sheet (1963

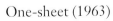

One-sheet (1963)

One-sheet (1965)

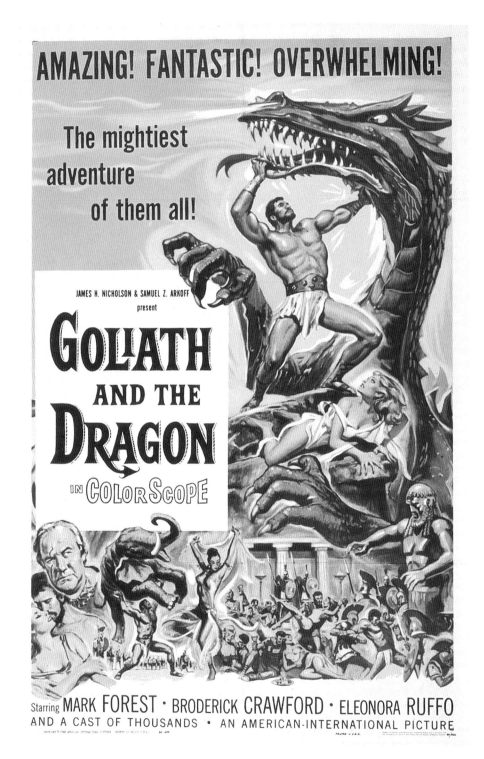

One-sheet (1960)

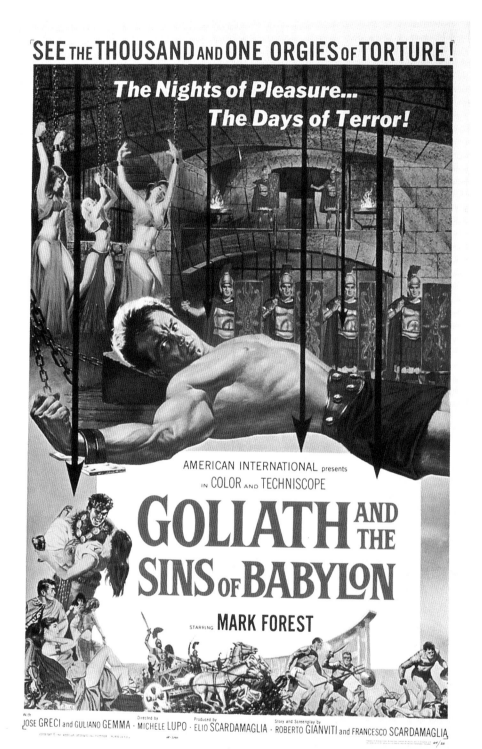

One-sheet (1964)

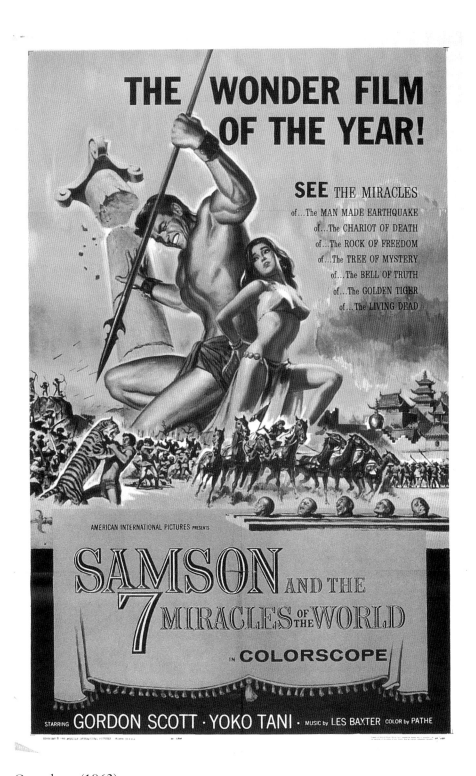

One-sheet (1962)

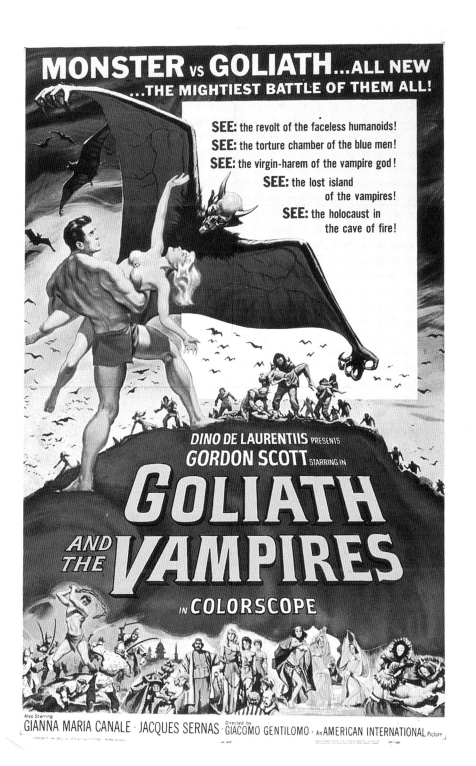

One-sheet (1964)

143

One-sheet (1959)

One-sheet (1961)

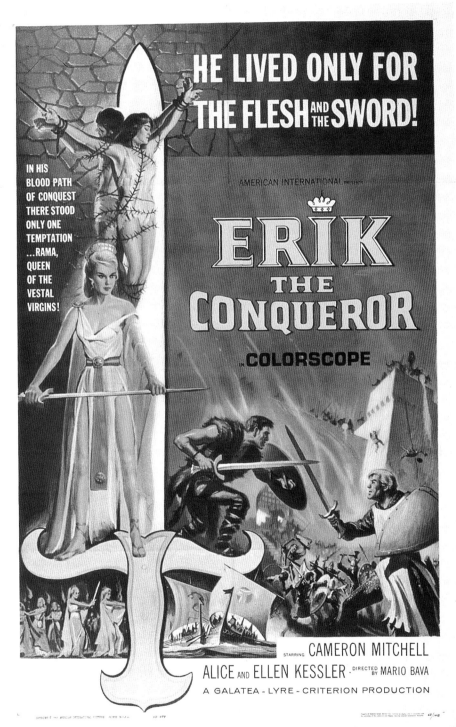

One-sheet (1962)

One-sheet (1962)

Italian poster
(1960—U.S. title: *Robin Hood and the Pirates*)

Italian poster
(1963—U.S. title: *The Lion of St. Mark*)

Italian poster
(1964—U.S. title: *Sandokan the Great*)

Italian poster
(1962—U.S. title: *The Trojan Horse*)

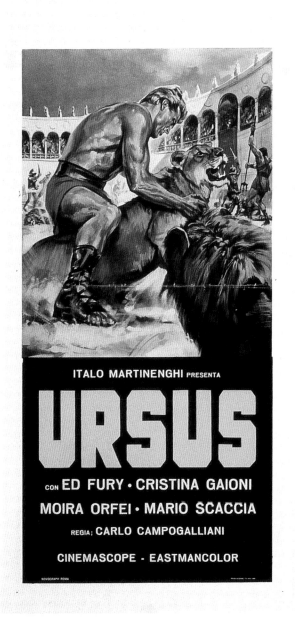

Italian poster
(1964 reissue—U.S. title: *The Mighty Ursus*)

Italian poster
(1964 reissue—U.S. title: *Hercules Against Rome*)

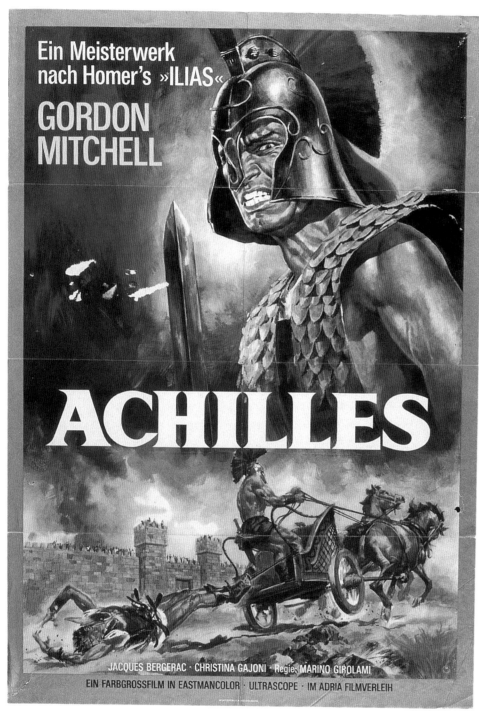

German poster
(1962—U.S. release undetermined)

German poster
(1964—U.S. title: *The Avenger*)

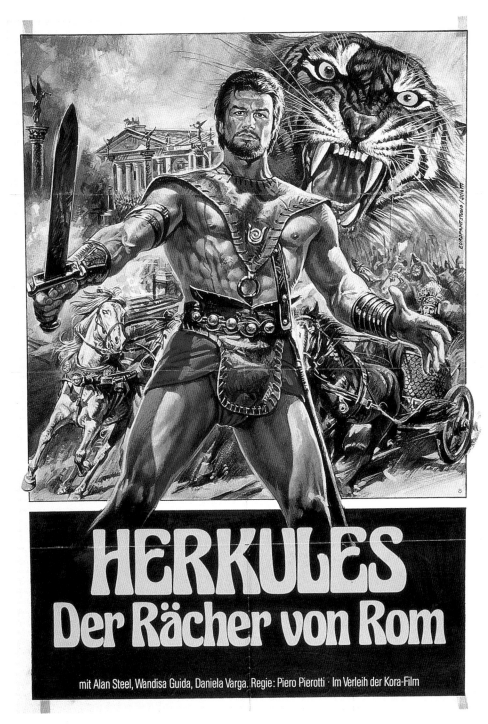

German poster
(1960—U.S. title: *Hercules Against Rome*)

German poster
(1961—U.S. title: *The Giant of Metropolis*)

BIBLIOGRAPHY

Arkoff, Sam. *Flying Through Hollywood By the Seat of My Pants.* New York: Birch Lane Press, 1992.

Balio, Tino. *United Artists—The Company That Changed The Film Industry.* Wisconsin: The University of Wisconsin Press, 1987.

Bassoff, Lawrence. "Hercules: Back to the Stables," *Los Angeles Times.* March 28, 1978.

———. "Miklos Rozsa: 150 Fanfares From an Uncommon Man," *Los Angeles Times.* December 28, 1979.

———. "Sunset Hovers Over the Paramount Ranch," *Los Angeles Times.* February 6, 1980.

Behlmer, Rudy. *Inside Warner Bros.* New York: Viking Press, 1985.

———. Memo from Darryl F. Zanuck. New York: Grove Press, 1993.

Belton, John. *Widescreen Cinema.* Massachusetts: Harvard University Press, 1992.

Brown, Gene. *Movie Time.* New York: Macmillan, 1995.

Carnes, Mark C. *Past Imperfect—History According to the Movies.* New York: Henry Holt and Company, Inc. 1995.

Cary, John. *Spectacular!—The Story of Epic Films.* London: Hamlyn, 1974

Christian, Linda. *Linda—My Own Story.* New York: Crown Publishers, 1962.

Cowie, Peter. *A Concise History of The Cinema.* London: A. Zwemmer Limited, 1971.

Custen, George F. *Bio/Pics—How Hollywood Constructed Public History.* New Jersey: Rutgers University Press, 1992.

Drabble, Margaret. *The Oxford Companion to English Literature.* Oxford: Oxford University Press, 1985.

Dupuy, R. Ernest and Trevor Dupuy. *The Harper Encyclopedia of Military History.* New York: Harper Collins Publishers, 1993.

Edwards, Anne. *The DeMilles—An American Family.* London: Collins, 1988.

Essoe, Gabe and Raymond Lee. *DeMille—The Man and His Pictures.* Cranbury: A. S. Barnes, 1970.

Flynn, Errol. *My Wicked, Wicked Ways.* New York: G. P. Putnam's Sons, 1959.

Fraser, George MacDonald. *The Hollywood History of the World.* London: The Harvill Press, 1991.

Granger, Stewart. *Sparks Fly Upward.* New York: G. P. Putnam's Sons, 1981.

Guiles, Fred Lawrence. *Tyrone Power—The Last Idol.* Garden City: Doubleday and Company, 1979.

Herman, Jan. *A Talent for Trouble—The Life of Hollywood's Most Acclaimed Director, William Wyler.* New York: G. P. Putnam's Sons, 1995.

Herndon, Booton. *Mary Pickford and Douglas Fairbanks.* New York: W. W. Norton and Company Inc., 1977.

Higham, Charles. *Cecil B. DeMille—A Biography of the Most Successful Film Maker of Them All.* New York: Charles Scribner's Sons, 1973

———. *Errol Flynn The Untold Story.* Garden City: Doubleday and Company, 1980.

Hirschhorn, Clive. *The Universal Story.* London: Octopus Books Limited, 1983.

Hopp, Glenn. *VideoHound's Epics—Giants of the Big Screen.* Detroit, London: Visible Ink Press, 1999.

Julius, Marshall. *Action! The Action Movie A–Z.* Bloomington and Indianapolis: Indiana University Press, 1996.

Karlin, Fred. *Listening To Movies.* New York: Schirmer Books, 1994.

Kinnard, Roy. *The Blue and The Gray on the Silver Screen—More Than 80 Years of Civil War Movies.* Toronto: Carol Publishing Group, 1996.

———. *The Warner Bros. Story.* New York: Crown Publishers, Inc., 1979.

Maeder, Edward. *Hollywood and History: Costume Design in Film.* Los Angeles: Los Angeles County Museum of Art, 1987.

Mast, Gerald. *A Short History of the Movies.* New York: Macmillan Publishing Company, 1986.

Meyer, William R. *Warner Brothers Directors.* New Rochelle: Arlington House, 1978.

The New York Times. The New York Times Film Reviews, Volumes 2–6. New York: The New York Times and Arno Press, 1970.

Parish, James Robert and Don E. Stanke. *The Swashbucklers.* New Jersey: Rainbow Books, 1976.

Perkins, George, Barbara Perkins, and Philip Leininger (eds.) *Benet's Reader's Encyclopedia of American Literature.* New York: Harper Collins, 1991.

Sauter, Michael. *The Worst Movies of All Time.* New York: Carol Publishing Group, 1995.

Schatz, Thomas. *The Genius of The System—Hollywood Filmmaking in the Studio Era.* New York: Henry Holt and Company, 1988.

Shipman, David. *The Great Movie Stars—The Golden Years.* New York: Bonanza Books, 1970.

———. *The Great Movie Stars—The International Years.* New York: St. Martin's Press, Inc., 1972.

Sinclair, Andrew. *Spiegel—The Man Behind The Pictures.* Boston and Toronto: Little, Brown and Company, 1987.

Smith, Gary A. *Epic Films.* Jefferson, NC: McFarland and Company, Inc., 1991.

Stockham, Martin. *The Korda Collection.* London: Boxtree, 1992.

Taves, Brian. *The Romance of Adventure.* Jackson: University Press of Mississippi, 1993.

Thomas, Tony. *Cads and Cavaliers.* New York: A. S. Barnes and Co. Inc., 1973.

———. *The Great Adventure Films.* Secaucus, NJ: Citadel Press, 1976.

———, Rudy Behlmer, Clifford McCarty. *The Films of Errol Flynn.* New York: The Citadel Press, 1969.

Vasey, Ruth. *The World According to Hollywood—1918–1939.* Wisconsin: The University of Wisconsin Press, 1997.

Weisser, Thomas. *Spaghetti Westerns—The Good, The Bad, and The Violent.* Jefferson, NC: McFarland and Company, Inc., 1992.

Willis, Donald C. *The Films of Howard Hawks.* New Jersey: The Scarecrow Press, Inc., 1975.

German AO poster
(1960—U.S. title: *Son of Samson*)

INDEX OF MOVIE POSTERS